PRAISE FOR *INTO THE SPOTLIGHT*

Into the Spotlight is powerful, forceful, honest, reassuring and creates a belief that 'I can do this'. Nicola Moras has broken everything down into achievable steps and makes it all feel possible.

Kim Fullager | Boss Lady at The Mind Master

Nicola Moras chooses to write her own story and unapologetically walk – or should I say swagger – full pelt into it. Unlike so many with an online following, brand, or influence, who show up as a confident bad-ass of sorts, Nicola is one of the few who bares her soul and is consistently unafraid to show up.

It is extraordinarily rare to find a person so deeply dedicated to walking their true path, and guiding others to do the same so successfully.

You absolutely can and *must* step into the spotlight and do the work you were born to do. This book gives you the opportunity to learn from Nicola. It just might change your life.

Katrina Ruth | Kicking the Ass of the 1% Within the 1% at The Katrina Ruth Show

This is a must-read book for anyone who knows that they need to create a powerful personal brand. Stepping *Into the Spotlight* has never been more important than it is today. In order to cut through the noise online and be seen as different, you really do need to follow everything Nicola says and just do it! It should be required reading for all business owners.

Gerda Muller | Clinical psychologist and private practice success business coach and mentor

If you are in the business of helping other people you need to be visible, and in order to be visible, you have to step into the spotlight. What I love about what Nicola teaches is the importance of being YOU while you're doing this. Nicola makes it easy for you to reach more of the people you love working with, in a way that is ethical, powerful and and makes you shine.

Jo Muirhead | Chief Life Changer at JoMuirhead.com and PurpleCo

Nicola is a walking, talking advertisement for how business owners need to step into the spotlight and be visible. She doesn't mince words and only shares the things that work! *Into the Spotlight* is a manual for how to get out of your own way and own your piece of the internet. If you want to reach more people in a way that is authentic, real and with no BS, then you must read this book.

Tess Crawley | CEO The Crawley Clinic, psychologist and business coach

I love how Nicola makes it simple for you to see the importance of stepping into your own spotlight. She teaches you step by step, holding your hand the whole way. I highly recommend everyone read this book!

Rachael O'Connor | Clinical director and principal psychologist BSc (Psych) Grad Dip (Psych), MAPS, STAP

INTO THE
SPOTLIGHT

NICOLA MORAS

ACKNOWLEDGEMENTS

I wanted to start my book by acknowledging YOU! Without you, the entrepreneur who wants to change the world, this book would not be possible. I want to acknowledge your bravery, your tenacity and your persistence in making your business work through your marketing and visibility. The world truly needs more people like you who are willing to put themselves out there, to be vulnerable and show their awesomeness to the world. You rock, my friend!

They say it takes a village to raise a child, and I have to share with you that it's the same to grow a business – and write a book, of course! I'd love it if you would join me in celebrating the following RAD humans who have made it possible for this book to come to life and, honestly, for helping me stay somewhat sane since 2010 when I started this business.

I want to say a huge thank you to my parents, my grandparents and my aunties for modelling entrepreneurship to me for as long as I can remember. You have always shown an active interest in personal and professional growth, coaching and looking for ways to make the world better. To Mum and Dad for showing me and my brother, while we were growing up, that when you are tenacious and relentless in your pursuit of living the best possible life, it's all possible. Thank you for your love and support and for tirelessly cheering me on.

A big hug of gratitude has to go to Jo Muirhead, my bestie, cheerleader, butt kicker, advocate and truth slayer! This woman has shown endless grace and grit, humility and humour since I have known her. This woman is the poster child for resilience and it's such a pleasure and joy to be her friend! Thank you, Jo, for a-l-w-a-y-s being there for me at my lowest of lows and highest of highs, and everywhere in between. I don't think I'd still be in business if it weren't for you.

I am endlessly grateful to both my current personal mentors and other mentors over the years – from my first mentor Amber McLean, to Leela Cosgrove and Gulliver Giles, to Kevin Nations, Toby Alexander, Janine Garner, Kelly Irving and Katrina Ruth. I am grateful to all the people who have written books over the years who have helped inform, educate, motivate and inspire me. Without you all, I would not be where I am. Thank you.

Please put your hands together for my clients! You all rock! I am so grateful to be a part of your worlds and witness to your growth, courage, vulnerability and trust. I love seeing you show up in the world in the most amazing ways, helping, inspiring and motivating so many people. I am in awe of you.

Thanks to Major Street – in particular Lesley – for picking up this book. I am so excited to see what happens with this! To the editors, designers, book layout geniuses, thank you! To my publicist extraordinaire Scott Eathorne for introducing us – what a team.

To my children Tiana, Ezrie and Jake. Thank you for being my amazing 'little' humans! I love you all more than I can put into words and I hope I do you proud. I imagine it's not easy being the children of someone who strives every day to grow. But heck, would you rather a 'boring' life?

Last, but far the least, to my husband Dom. Gosh, what a ride, Babe! Thank you for being so damn happy (most of the time) to support me and ride beside me during this 'Crazy Little Thing Called Love'! There have been so many twists and turns and I couldn't ask for someone to do any more than you have done! I love you, truly, madly deeply (with a nod to Savage Garden, naturally).

Finally, back to you, the reader. Thank you! Without you, there'd be no book. The world really does need you, your awesomeness, your brilliance, your wit, your sass, your knowledge, your fire, your passion and your personality.

It's time to step into the spotlight, my friend.

You rock. I can't wait to see you shine.

First published in 2020 by Major Street Publishing Pty Ltd
PO Box 106, Highett, Vic. 3190
 E | info@majorstreet.com.au
 W | majorstreet.com.au
 M | +61 421 707 983

© Nicola Moras 2020

The moral rights of the author have been asserted.

A catalogue record for this
book is available from the
National Library of Australia

ISBN: 978-0-6487963-2-9

Cover design by Tess McCabe
Internal design by Production Works
Printed in Australia by Ovato, an Accredited ISO AS/NZS 14001:2004 Environmental Management System Printer.

10 9 8 7 6 5 4 3 2 1

CONTENTS

FOREWORD
BY JANINE GARNER

Eight years ago, I was sitting in a café, across from a small business owner. I listened carefully as this business owner shared her journey from starting out in her own front room to now having three skincare clinics in her town. There was no doubt she was doing well and had already achieved great results. There was equally no doubt in my mind that she could see the possibility of a new frontier of brilliance that would involve playing a bigger game, but her inner voices of doubt were creeping in. *'I'm not sure I can, Janine.' 'Do you really think it's possible?' 'Am I good enough?'*

'Yes, Yes, Yes', I kept saying.

It was time to take action. With lunch ordered, a sneaky glass of bubbles on the side and pens and paper everywhere, we mapped out the landscape, the strategic plan, the long-term vision versus the quick wins and a connection and communication strategy that would increase her visibility and help her scale her business and reach new levels.

A year later, she launched her first clinic interstate, embarked on a profile-building marketing campaign and went on to become a Telstra Award-winning business owner. I've remained connected to her over the years and watched from the sidelines as her business and profile grew, as she sold the business and as she evolved into the next stage of her personal journey. When I asked her about her learnings, she said, *'I have learnt two key things: firstly reciprocity, to share knowledge freely and expect nothing in return, and secondly to stand out — be brave and bold'*.

Ultimately, we all have to get better at being ourselves, at finding the courage to step into our brilliance to shine. My own journey, like many, has been one of significant highs and horrendous lows; of high-five moments and days when I wanted to hide under the doona. I've tackled the ongoing, exhausting battle between striving for more and proving I was good enough, of battling self-doubt and the voices telling me I wasn't smart enough, savvy enough, brave enough or good enough.

Instead of staying invisible, I rose to the challenge, I faced fear and pushed through. I surrounded myself with an inner circle of confidantes who believed in me and pushed me to become more, and I knew that the only way I could achieve my dreams was to own them, to take the right action and to be courageous and brave enough to stand in my spotlight and shine.

Since then, I've risen through the ranks corporately for some of the world's best brands, built and sold my own business, launched a not-for-profit and raised thousands of dollars to help disadvantaged women and kids in our own backyard. I've written three books, received an Honorary Doctorate of Science and I now travel the world speaking and training individuals in organisations to unleash their own brilliance in how they connect, collaborate and lead.

Remaining invisible isn't being brilliant.

Doing nothing isn't being brilliant.

Taking action and choosing to own your uniquely individual spotlight is brilliant. It will take you to a place where you are noticed for the work you are doing, fired up to do more. It is what will take you from dreaming a dream to living your dream.

The world needs you to be your exceptional self. It needs you to step up and trust that in that amazing body and mind of yours exists your inner brilliance.

You have all you need.

It's up to you to decide if you are ready.

In this book, Nicola Moras is going to take you through why it's so important for you to step in to and own your spotlight. Not only that, you'll learn how to do that with gusto and confidence, so the whole world gets to see you, your brilliance and your mastery. As she says, *'The world is ready for your brand of awesome'*.

It's time to jump in.

Janine Garner
Best-selling author and international keynote speaker

PREFACE

Imagine for a moment that you're backstage at the 1985 Live Aid concert. You're about to go on stage and do what you do best, in front of tens of thousands of people (not to mention the millions who are watching on television).

You have a moment before you set out on stage, when you remember back to where you started. You've worked so hard to get to this point. There was a time when you could only dream of the exposure that you would have: the following, the influence, the thousands of people who could speak your words as if they were you. You pinch yourself. How did you get so lucky? You can hear, see and feel the energy of the audience, even though you're not on stage yet. It feels like magic. Your arms are goose-pimply. Your senses are heightened and you know you are ready.

You look back and do a quick stocktake of all that you've done. You're so proud of yourself, for working through the trials and tribulations, for learning how to make your dreams happen.

If the eighties weren't your decade, you could imagine that Lady Gaga must have felt like this before stepping on to multiple stages to receive her many awards, while standing up for those who had been bullied, abused, downtrodden and made to feel worthless.

Or you could imagine that this is how Jennifer Lopez felt, waiting under the stage, ready to be hoisted up on the rising platform at the 2020 Super Bowl.

Imagine being able to have that level of impact, to have a voice that could reach millions of people globally.

We all know of Freddie Mercury, the original lead singer of Queen. Whether you like Queen as a band or not, you have to admit that they have had a massive influence in the music industry with their innovative and uncompromising sound. They've played their message through their music.

Queen's commitment to their own style and way of doing things led to their music still being enjoyed in the 2020s by fans of all ages – from 11-year-olds to those in their seventies and eighties. Movies have been made about them, books written about them and even a stadium tour created in their honour in 2020, with Adam Lambert as lead singer. They still have 'it'. Imagine being able to fill stadiums with fans, five decades into your career?

Queen embraced their uniqueness. They embraced their points of difference. They decided that they would just be themselves and that people could either get on board or not.

You may not have the reach yet, nor the notoriety, to pull off the equivalent of your own Live Aid performance, but that doesn't mean it can't or won't happen. You have to get past your own limiting beliefs about what you can and can't do. You have to stop worrying whether people will like you. (Yes, that's a thing.)

> Truth bomb: many people won't like you! Sorry (not sorry).
> It's a fact.

You can do everything 'right' and there will still be people who don't like you.

So, you need to be clear on how you can step into your own spotlight, and reach the audience(s) who do want to hear from you and learn from you. Then you get on with the job at hand *without* being boring and generic – because that will keep you hidden.

WHY YOU NEED TO STEP INTO THE SPOTLIGHT

Being visible in the online world today is crucial if you want to make it in business or in your career. More and more business owners are embracing social media and starting to rely heavily on the unique leverage that it offers. But most of them don't have the confidence to step into their spotlight. Let's be honest, social media is noisy and, quite frankly, it can seem futile to think about populating the platforms with even more content. I mean, who's going to pay attention?

Many people suffer from 'imposter syndrome'. This is when they have qualifications coming out of their ears, and a whole lot of life experience, but they still feel like a fraud. I've seen people with more than 20 legitimate qualifications and they think they don't know enough – until they go through what I'm going to share with you in this book, of course!

You don't want your business to be under threat in the same way that a lot of brick-and-mortar businesses are right now. We've all witnessed major stores going into liquidation. Big brands we thought would be around forever and stand the test of time are gone – primarily because they couldn't remain competitive in the online world. Don't be one of them!

Although becoming visible is not a quick fix or magic pill to business prosperity and longevity, there is a process to it. I see it as a four-step Entrepreneurs Quest for Visibility. The process takes you from:

1. singing in the shower, being afraid of anyone hearing you and seeing you; to

2. busking at any venue that will book you, then becoming clear about where you want to be heard and by whom; to

3. owning your inner rock star; to

4. nailing it and moving on to your version of Live Aid.

After step 4, you are creating *influence*. You get to do what you want, where you want and how you want to do it, in a way that leverages you and your unique message, skills and talents.

In this book, I guide you through the four steps showing you how to:

► gain **confidence**

► find your **hot coal clients**™

► develop your **uniqueness**, voice and positioning

► become **visible** and make your business **thrive**.

If you don't go through these four stages, you run the risk of staying stuck singing in the shower forever, and nobody will know who the heck you are. In fact, do you even exist if you're not online? (Just kidding.)

You don't want to be busking out there at every venue, every night of the week, either. In the online world, this looks like trying to spend time, money and energy on every single platform and it leads to exhaustion and confusion, and most people throw in the towel declaring it a big fat waste of time.

You cannot afford to be on every platform all the time, trying to build connections and conversations with everyone. It takes a superhuman effort and, as a business owner, you are time poor. You've got a family, animals, friends, sports, book clubs and champagne nights (oh wait, maybe that's just me!). The point is, you've got other shit to do and you don't want (or need) to be spending more time than necessary online. You have to be super-specific about *who* you're talking to, *where* you're talking to them and *how* you're talking to them, so that you are heard. Your audience wants to feel valued, to know you understand them and what they're going through – and that you can help.

In this book I teach you how to:

- stand out in the crowd;
- own your point of difference; and
- articulate that in a way that makes sense to your audience, your people, your fans and followers (and, oh, how they will love you for it).

From there you're going to work through how to create influence and have that reach far and wide so that no matter where you are, people will connect with you, listen to you and take action on what you have to say.

'Oh, but Nicola, how the heck do I do all of this?' I hear you ask.

Don't worry, I've got your back! We're going to work through this step by step (à la NKOTB for my homies who were around in the eighties and nineties!) to make sure that you get all your magic out of your head and into an actionable plan.

Then, it's up to you to implement said plan and do the work – to show up and step into your spotlight. You'll take charge of the future that you want to create for yourself, your family, your friends and your audience.

I'm going to make the plan super-simple for you to action. But, as with anything and everything, knowledge without action is great for the brain but it won't produce results. Without action, you'll be left singing in the metaphorical shower or busking for the entire business journey that you've embarked on and, honestly, that would be devastating. Nobody wants to own a Chanel bag and have it sit in the cupboard never to see the light of day.

The world needs you. They are ready for you. They are ready for your brand of awesomeness.

Shall we get stuck into it?

ONE
THE TIME
IS NOW

IMAGINE FOR A MOMENT you are Freddie Mercury at the start of the movie *Bohemian Rhapsody*, standing in the bar, watching the band perform on stage. You know in your heart of hearts that it should be you up there on that stage performing. You stand against the wall and breathe in the familiar old-time bar smells of beer, wine and wood.

You smile to yourself as you watch the band play. It's a bit of a double-edged sword being in the audience there in that moment. You're enjoying what you're listening to but, at the same time, you're also imagining yourself up there performing, having fun, doing your thing. You imagine what you'd do differently. You've known since you were a child that you're different, special; that you were going to make it and live a life less ordinary.

As your thoughts drift from scenario to scenario, you imagine what it must be like out there in the spotlight, with all eyes on you. People are watching you and singing along to *your* songs. You look around the room and see smiles on people's faces as they sing, dance and connect with the musicians on stage as well as with each other. It's as if everyone is moving as one big, connected organism.

You snap out of it for a moment and wonder if you'll ever truly make it into the spotlight – and what that would entail.

The set finishes. You make your way out through the back of the bar to the laneway to discover the band has lost its lead singer. You pitch to the band members on why you should sing for them... and you're in! You're on your way. Yes, you have your doubts: *'What if it doesn't work? What if I can't get along with the other band members? What if it all fails? What if the audience doesn't like me and prefers the other guy? Have I got enough experience? I'm flamboyant, what if they don't get it?'*

I am certain that these thoughts would have been going through Freddie's head, but as they say 'the rest is history' – well, for Freddie, anyway!

EMBRACE YOUR FEAR

When most people think about putting themselves 'out there' on social media they get caught up with doubt and fear. They worry about public perception. They stress about what to say and when. They want to make sure that they're not about to undermine the credibility and the goodwill they've created already when they start to do more online. *'Is it worth it? Am I worth it? What if I screw it all up?'*

But, like Freddie, you have to embrace the fear and do it anyway. Approach the band and see if they want a new lead singer! Imagine that band is your online audience and you are the lead singer. You are the person who's going to be front and centre, come hell or high water – owning it! You are the personality; the rock star.

I'm sure there were other people in that bar who were also imagining themselves up on the stage, being the lead singer or the drummer or the guitarist. Musicians and singers have a way of making their performances look so easy, and this inspires audiences to want to be up there in their place. It's the reason live concerts sell out. It's why some people show up dressed as the artist they're about to see, or wearing the band's t-shirts. They feel inspired by them and want to be part of the magic that the artists bring to the table.

Everyone in business these days is looking for a way to stand out. They're looking to cut through the noise: to be seen and heard.

In the digital world, the last thing anyone wants to be doing is fighting for the scraps. The people who are in the spotlight will get the attention and, honestly, you simply cannot afford to ignore this and be left behind.

It's a little like being the best singer in the world but only singing in the shower. (I talk about this more in chapter 4.) Singing in the shower carries no risk. There's nothing to be afraid of because nobody other than your family can hear your fabulous voice. But, if it's amazing – like that of an angel – it deserves to be out there and unleashed on the world! If not, you'll remain the world's best-kept secret.

I'm not talking about you pretending to be Freddie Mercury, or anyone else. I'm talking about you stepping into the spotlight and claiming your rightful place online – in your own way, with your own sense of flair and personality.

Why? Because your future depends on it.

You need to stand out and be seen by those who should be working with you. Being visible online by creating – and stepping into – your own spotlight means that your potential clients will see you. They will get to know you; they'll learn to like you and they'll definitely trust you. Trust paves the way for you to grow your client base and business beyond anything you've ever dreamed of.

BE YOURSELF – EVERYONE ELSE IS TAKEN

You're going to show up online in all of your glory, showcasing *you*, your personality and your knowledge, which will meet your clients' needs and improve their lives.

I loved the scene in *Bohemian Rhapsody* where Queen met with their first manager; they told him that they create music for the 'weirdos' in the corner, because they, too, are weirdos and misfits. They wanted to create a sense of belonging and community – a way to share the experience with others so they didn't feel so damn alone.

People like me and you don't want to be or feel ordinary. We never have and we never will. We've always felt a bit weird, as if we don't belong. But, guess what? The more we talk about this – the more we share our 'not-belonging-ness' – the more others will admit that they feel the same way. That's when we start to create a community and a place for all of us who are odd to be odd together! It's liberating and helps us feel as if we have somewhere we belong.

Humans have a basic need to belong and to connect with each other. But, many people online are feeling more and more disconnected on a daily basis, which is incredibly ironic given that social media and digital platforms are the very things trying to build connection. People are slower to trust these days because there are too many fakes, frauds and people selling snake oil online.

What are you supposed to do? You know you need to use social media to grow your businesses. You know you need to connect with your people. The most important and powerful thing that you can ever do is to be yourself online.

It's crucial you show up and help people to see you, and to see that you are a truth teller; that you are the leader that they have been hoping to find. They are silently begging to find someone they can relate to and connect with; they want a real human on the other side of their screens who they feel they can trust.

It's definitely going to take some work on your part to become this trusted person online. The digital space is like a crowded stadium, where everyone's voices are drowning out everyone else's. You have to find a way to stand out. You have to become the rock star of your own industry.

THE EVOLUTION OF A STAR

To become that trusted online presence – to be visible and claim your rightful rock star status – is an evolutionary, seven-step process.

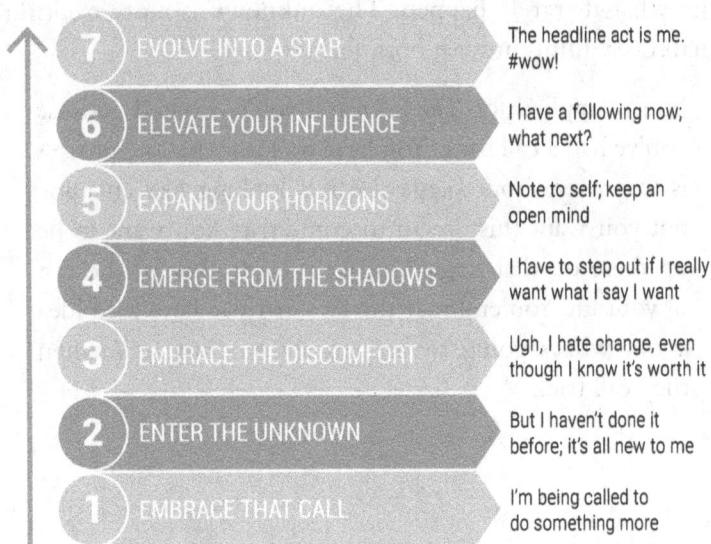

Step		Thought
7	EVOLVE INTO A STAR	The headline act is me. #wow!
6	ELEVATE YOUR INFLUENCE	I have a following now; what next?
5	EXPAND YOUR HORIZONS	Note to self; keep an open mind
4	EMERGE FROM THE SHADOWS	I have to step out if I really want what I say I want
3	EMBRACE THE DISCOMFORT	Ugh, I hate change, even though I know it's worth it
2	ENTER THE UNKNOWN	But I haven't done it before; it's all new to me
1	EMBRACE THAT CALL	I'm being called to do something more

I'm going to work through this process with you, step by step.

Step 1 – Embrace that call

The first step is to embrace the call to be brave and vulnerable; to show up online, to be you, to step into the spotlight.

> You're in the shower and your partner tells you that you're the best singer. On this occasion you choose to believe them. They mention that there's an audition for *The Voice* coming up and you should apply. You vomit in your mouth a little and say 'okay', because you know it's time. This is what you were born for.

Step 2 – Enter the unknown

So many people just don't do this because they're deathly afraid of the what-ifs: from the haters on the internet to things not working out. Well, I've got news for you, honey: the what-ifs rarely happen. The unknown is more exciting than ever! Jump in with both feet.

> You've applied for *The Voice* and you're excited because you've had a call back. You have no idea what the process is from here. Your biggest fear is looking like an idiot, but you want this dream to come true. You want to be up there on that stage. You want to do this for the rest of your life. You embrace the fact that you have zero idea about what's going to happen and you say 'yes' when they call back.

Step 3 – Embrace the discomfort

Nothing good comes from staying in your comfort zone. It's when you're out of your comfort zone that the magic happens.

At *The Voice* auditions you are super-scared. You've never sung in front of an audience before (the bathroom towels don't count!). You feel nervous, you have butterflies in your stomach, but you remind yourself that you've got this. You *can* do this. And you change your self-talk to being supportive... of yourself!

Step 4 – Emerge from the shadows

I know it can feel safe in the shadows, but nothing grows in the dark except moss and mould. You don't want that. It's time to emerge from the shadows and step into the light – your spotlight.

You're backstage at the first live auditions for *The Voice*. You're standing there, sweaty and nervous, wondering if the microphone is going to slide out of your hands. They call your name and you take a deep breath. You walk out onto the stage and into the spotlight. And you sing as if your life depends on it.

Step 5 – Expand your horizons

This is where you start to look at what you're doing with an open mind. In order to get to somewhere you've never been, you have to do things you've never done.

You've made it through the entire competition and you're in the final eight. You're feeling as if this is all a dream! You're so excited but, again, you find yourself in a space where you have no idea what's going to happen or how! You know you're doing your very best – as is everyone else. The thing that you're beginning to realise is that so many more opportunities have started to make themselves known to you. You realise that no matter the outcome of the show, you'll be great and you'll find a way to do what you love.

Step 6 – Elevate your influence

At this point, you're able to share your own thoughts and opinions on pretty much anything and everything and people are listening. You've built up a following and that's really exciting! You have people who love you!

The Voice is over and you won! You're so grateful that you got through and that the audience out there has backed you. You know that there are genuine people who love your voice. You are now able to really start singing your own music and playing your own tunes. This means that you can start to sing more of the songs that mean something to you, and to your audience.

Step 7 – Evolve into a star

When you get to this stage, you have turned from a caterpillar into a butterfly and you're finally owning the star quality that you have within.

When you truly become a star, you know that you can put on an event or a concert and people will come to see you as the headline act. You have stepped *fully* into the spotlight – your spotlight. You realise that, no matter what, you are amazing – and what you have to say will be heard by those who need to hear it.

When you have evolved through these seven steps, you are going to be *visible*. You are going to stand in your own spotlight and be recognised as someone who has something to say and something to contribute.

You'll automatically stand out from the crowd, because you're concerned only with being you; sharing your voice, leveraging your unique gifts, talents and knowledge to inspire, educate and entertain your audience. This creates recognition and you become famous for what you do professionally.

You've embraced your voice and you are exactly who you are. There's no faking it till you make it for you, my lovely! You're about to *rock it out!*

CASE STUDY: Jeromy and Kim

Jeromy and Kim started out with no audience online and very few sales. They were relying solely on referrals for their business, which helped to 'rewire children's brains for better learning'. They attended a workshop with me in 2014 as a 'last-ditch effort' to try to use Facebook for their business.

They had a string of 'failed' businesses behind them and their confidence had dwindled. They were starting to lose their passion for their business, and were tempted to give up on their dream to leave their day jobs and work together in their business full time.

They worked through the evolution of a star process and they now have tens of thousands of people who follow them and watch their content. Their audience – their hot coal clients – love them. (I'll tell you more about hot coal clients in chapter 5.)

THE POWER OF THE SPOTLIGHT

Social media is growing at a rapid rate, and you must embrace it if you want to grow your business. Facebook alone has an audience of 2.61 billion people, and half of those are on the platform daily and on mobile.

We've seen people with influence use their platforms on social media to great effect. For example, Australian comedian Celeste Barber rallied the support of her online community at home and overseas to raise funds for those who really needed it during the devastating bushfires in late 2019 and early 2020. She was able to raise millions of dollars because she had built a powerful online profile by just being herself.

When you have stepped into the spotlight, you can influence those around you to your way of thinking. By educating and entertaining them, you help them to see that they, too, can be themselves.

By stepping into your spotlight, you naturally inspire others to step into theirs.

CHAPTER SUMMARY

THE TIME IS NOW.

EMBRACE YOUR FEAR.

BE YOURSELF.

TWO

IT'S TIME TO MAKE AN IMPACT

I REMEMBER GOING to the funeral of my grandfather when I was in my early twenties. I was heartbroken. My grandfather and I shared the same birthday so, naturally, I felt a special affinity between the two of us. As clearly as I can remember what I did yesterday, I remember him coming to my graduation from primary school, where I played the violin in front of the school. I remember looking out into the crowded room filled with parents and finding his face; he was beaming back at me. I could see the undeniable pride on his face and it made me feel as if I were the only person on earth!

My grandfather was a man who gave his heart and soul to his family and to his community. He was heavily involved in the swimming programs at the community pool. He was always there, always present. He talked to everyone. He would stir them up and generally created a welcoming, warm and friendly atmosphere for the hundreds of students who would come through the centre on a weekly basis. He was cheeky and generous and a gentle giant.

He passed away suddenly from a heart aneurysm in 1999. It sent shockwaves through our family, and through the massive swimming communities that he had been involved in for decades.

When he died, hundreds of people turned out to pay their respects at his funeral. I played the violin as a way of honouring him (not well, I have to admit, as I tried to maintain composure amid floods of tears). I remember sitting in the front row, heartbroken, next to my heartbroken mother. It was a very sad day.

My grandfather was entrepreneurial by nature, which was quite brave in the 1990s. People were a lot more conservative then, unlike today when every human with a computer or a smartphone labels themselves as an entrepreneur!

He was always coming up with ideas and schemes and he was constantly on the lookout for opportunities to grow and build businesses. I recall one time when he returned from overseas with a pop-up tent. These did not exist at the time in Australia and he talked about importing them or having them made here under licence. We all thought he was crazy! My grandfather's name was William Ions. He was commonly called 'Bill Ions', which coincidentally combined to read 'BILLIONS'! It was in his name as well as his blood to create money from nothing but ideas.

The swim school and his family were my grandfather's passions. My aunty now runs the swim school. Under her mantle, it has evolved into a roaring success. Many of my family members have worked there and learned to swim there. It's as if my grandfather is in the water, still to this day, some 20 years on. His legacy continues.

My grandfather was brave. He was willing to do what it took to make things happen, even though it was against the 'norm'. I'm just so glad that I got to spend 21 years of my life knowing him, loving him and being part of his legacy.

He created a business that afforded him freedom, choice and flexibility, which is really what most of us want.

My grandfather didn't start to create his business until later on in life. But what if you don't have that long? None of us knows how much time we have. I'd advise you not to wait until your sixties to reinvent yourself. But if you have waited, get on to it now!

SEPARATING FACTS FROM FAILURE

Everyone in business aspires to create a business that affords them freedom, choice and flexibility; to be a respected leader in their industry, to create influence and change the lives of the people who they come in contact with. If you're reading this book, you're probably tarred with that same high-achieving brush.

You want to make your impact on the world.

Unlike in my grandfather's day, you have an amazing opportunity to reach the people who you want to help: you have social media to help you step into the spotlight. Yet, so many choose not to put themselves out there. So, I'm going to give you the facts:

- Social media has the broadest reach of any marketplace right now. People are becoming more and more reliant on the various social media platforms, using them for shopping and research and keeping in touch. Social media is *the* prime place for you to get your message out there.

- There is no better time than yesterday to get started on your quest for social media domination. (Okay, perhaps you're going more for social media *impact* rather than *domination*, but roll with me here!)

- If you really want what you say you want (to create freedom, choice and flexibility) then it's time for you to embrace the most accessible way of marketing to your audience, and that is to embrace social media.

- ► Every day that goes past you are closer to your death. (Too soon? I thought we were friends by now.) And that means that every day that goes past is one less day you have to reach the people who you want to help. Tough love, baby. It's how I roll!

- ► Every single business owner who *isn't* as visible as they want to be, needs to act *now*. You need to light a rocket under your butt and start getting yourself out there.

- ► Nobody is getting any younger. You don't know when the speeding social media train is going to come to a halt and the competition is only getting more and more fierce.

This is your wakeup call. Your future is waiting for you and your legacy isn't going to build itself.

We're all really good at believing that we are going to live forever. We all like to think that we're invincible and, at the same time, we know this is not true.

You have to create the confidence within to give it a go! You must get out there and try to make this work. (Don't worry, I'll step you through how to do that later in the book. You don't have to figure it out on your own.)

What's the worst thing that could happen? Honestly? Let's level with each other for a moment:

The worst thing that could happen is you might fail.

Gosh, I know, that would suck. But will you have learned something at the same time? Oh, hell yes!

You are smart, intelligent and I know that you do amazing things in this world already. If you look at how you have got to this point, I'm certain that every single thing in your life did not go according to plan. You've likely experienced rejection and proudly sport some battle scars.

You brushed yourself off (even if it took some time) and you got back on the horse. I know you did, because you're human and if you're reading this it's because at some point in your life you have failed at something. Even if it was as far back as learning to walk, you fell, you got back up and you had another try until you worked it out.

You've got this. Failure is normal and you should expect it to some degree. It's a consequence of trying something different.

OVERCOMING YOUR RESISTANCE

I've given you the facts about the power of social media and the opportunities it offers, but I'm still hearing your doubts. Let's look at these together.

You might look silly

Yes, you might, but we'll love you for it! And this stepping into the spotlight thing takes practice.

If I had a dollar for every time I thought I looked silly, I'd be a rich woman. This was one of my big concerns when I first started 'getting myself out there'. I was desperate to look and sound professional and when I look back at the things that I created when I first started, oh my gosh! I think I looked ridiculously silly! (Side note: if you want a chuckle, head over to my YouTube channel and take a look at the early videos I created. #cringe!) The magic happens when you worry about looking silly and do it anyway. We all have to start somewhere.

You could lose some 'credibility' in your industry

Yes, you might, but I suspect you won't; and, if you do, the people who decide to declare themselves the judge and jury of your visibility efforts are likely to be completely invisible, anyway. They'll be sitting on their high horses, wearing their judgey-mcjudgey pants, looking down their nose at you. But, secretly, they'll be wishing they had your confidence to get out there, talk about the things that are important and propel their legacy out into the world.

Don't worry. You've got this! You need to believe first and foremost in yourself. You need to be 100 per cent behind yourself and willing to give yourself permission to create *your* legacy – and this may mean you'll rattle a few cages of the judges along the way.

FROM IGNORANCE TO MASTERY

It's time for you to embrace change. As we know, humans have a love–hate relationship with change, and entrepreneurs and business owners do, too. It can be hard to leave behind the familiar, cosy comfort zone to embark on a whole new world, but I promise you this: you will not regret it, even for a moment. I'm going to explain how you can leave that cosy place of ignorance and make the changes to master your goals. I call this growing your muscle of mastery.

Muscle of mastery

LEVEL 6: Mastery
LEVEL 5: Consciously competent
LEVEL 4: The plateau
LEVEL 3: Awareness of your incompetence
LEVEL 2: Incompetence
LEVEL 1: Ignorance is not bliss

Level 1 – Ignorance is not bliss

Most of us lead an automated life. We get up, organise the children and/or ourselves, head to work, do what we do and head home. We have dinner, clean up, relax and hang out in whatever way we do that, head to bed and repeat – like groundhog day. We're quite oblivious to anything outside of our current reality. I call this operating at level 1 in the muscle of mastery. We are just blissfully unaware.

Often something happens that shakes us awake – a wakeup call, if you will – and we decide that something needs to shift. Perhaps you realise, with a start, that you've put on weight and *now* is the time that something needs to change. Or you might have realised that you are super-skinny and it's time to start to build some muscle and tone up. Either way, at this point, you decide that it's time to take action and get your butt to the gym.

In business, it could be that you realise that you've got to do something different to the way you've always done things if you want a different result.

As Einstein said, 'The definition of insanity is doing the same thing over and over again, but expecting different results'.

You've noticed that 'everyone' is online these days and, if you want to remain in business for the foreseeable future, you have to dance in the online world – even though it's a little uncomfortable. You know it's time. You've seen someone with less experience than you, and fewer qualifications, appear out of nowhere – and they're getting clients left, right and centre. So you decide to do something about it.

Level 2 – Incompetence

If you've ever been to a gym for the first time or after an extended break, you'll remember that the recovery from the session is fierce. By fierce, I do not mean fiercely amazing; I mean you end up in a world of pain with DOMS (delayed onset muscle soreness). I personally love this, because it tells me I've worked hard! It's the same in business: you'll be in pain when you start out and realise that there are a *lot* of muscles you haven't used in a really long time. You will feel conscious of being unfit, un-muscly and definitely not strong.

Level 3 – Awareness of your incompetence

At level 3 you have a heightened awareness of your incompetence. You laugh a bit at the fact that you fail to lift any of the weights (even the lightest ones) and you feel like a lightweight! You look around you and you're inspired by the others in the gym or the class. You tell yourself you've got this and you dig in a little deeper. You acknowledge to yourself that you're awesome for showing up and you're completely committed to making the changes that you want. You commit to practising. You commit to giving it your all, every time you go to the gym.

In business, this is where you start to put yourself out there. You're not really feeling comfortable and it's not as easy as you'd like. You also know, like at the gym, that knowledge and familiarity comes with practice. This is when it starts to become a little easier.

Level 4 – The plateau

As you move to level 4, the plateau, you know that you're doing okay. You've built some muscle, you're doing alright but you know that you're still playing a bit safe. It's become a little 'easy' and you coast along for a while. Then, out of the blue, someone comes into the room and they're lifting more than you. They're squatting lower than you and, suddenly, you find yourself becoming competitive! After all, if they can do it, you can do it! You've spent some time on the plateau enjoying the view, getting your breath, but now it's time to ramp it up.

In business, this is where you hit an income ceiling or a client ceiling. You think that this is perhaps as good as it gets. Then, you stumble across someone who is doing more than you with the same (or less) effort and you know that it's time to find another way to ramp things up. This is where you decide you have to step into the spotlight. You have to grow your online visibility. You have to do something to get the changes you want.

Level 5 – Consciously competent

By now, at the gym, you are very aware of your body. You know what it can handle and how much you can push. You're aware of how your body responds to different weights and different exercises. You're seeing great results and it gives you the push to keep going and to keep riding the momentum wave.

Like anything, it's actually getting a lot easier to follow what you need to do in order to get results. You are still aware of the work that you're doing, but you're also finding it doesn't take quite as much concentration or effort to get results. You haven't quite mastered all of the moves and the exercises, but you are close.

Congratulations! At this point you have become consciously competent. In business, this means your efforts to create content and increase your visibility no longer take the time they used to. You've found your voice. It's a lot easier to do what you need to do. It requires less thinking on your part and you're actually (gasp) enjoying the process.

Level 6 – Mastery

You're getting results. Your body has changed and you are so happy with what you're seeing in the mirror. You're feeling fit and strong; healthy and full of energy. You're also smart enough to know that if you take the foot off the pedal, or if you stop working the process, you could potentially slip back to where you were before. The payoff here is that it's all a heck of a lot easier for you to maintain the results that you have – you have built the muscle of mastery.

In business, this is where you do what you need to do without really thinking about it too hard. You've mastered the art of building your confidence. You've mastered the art of communication. You've nailed the way you show up and you're out there doing it every single day.

YOUR IMPACT IS YOUR LEGACY

What you want to build and create is important. You and I both know this. I am sure you want to grow and expand your visibility because you want to help more people with what you do. You'd like to leave a legacy of empowerment for your clients, your family, your children and your friends. What you want to do is change the world.

The work that you do is important and the more you can grow your visibility, the more people you'll be able to help. There's a beautiful thing that happens then, and it's this: helping one person by doing what you do has a profound impact on the people around *them*. All of a sudden, it's not just one person that you're having an impact on, it's all the people around *them*, which then ripples out to the people around them. Your work will (and does) change and help endless numbers of people.

What more of a legacy could any of us really want to create and leave behind after we're gone?

Just as my grandfather's legacy has impacted his children and grandchildren, I know that it will have an impact on his great- and great-great-grandchildren, and beyond.

✳ ACTIVITY: *Future you, now*

Have you ever thought about why you're doing what you're doing? It's very important to calibrate and align yourself with what you want – both now and in the future. There's a common saying: *'what you focus on is what you get'*. A great activity to find this focus is what I call my 'future you, now' activity.

Imagine that you have everything you want: the results, clients, money, visibility, credibility and reputation in your industry. Write down what all that looks like as if it's already happened.

What are people telling you? How are you feeling? Where are you living? What are you telling yourself? What are you even doing in this 'ideal day' that you've got in your head? How does this tie into the legacy that you want to leave? I want you to make this feel as real as possible; sit in it, close your eyes and smell your future. Taste it, hear it, absorb it.

This 'future you, now' activity is something I personally use regularly to remain aligned and on track. It helps me push through the plateaus and the dips in my motivation. Every mentor who I have worked with uses something similar to recalibrate, reinvigorate and propel themselves forward.

Tony Robbins says, *'Where focus goes, energy flows'*. This activity will help you continue to focus on what you want so the energy to achieve it can flow.

Make sure you listen to the visualisation that goes along with this at: www.nicolamoras.com.au/intothespotlight

CHAPTER SUMMARY

KNOW THE FACTS ABOUT THE POWER OF SOCIAL MEDIA.

STEP UP FROM IGNORANCE TO ACHIEVE THE MUSCLE OF MASTERY.

WHAT IS THE LEGACY YOU'D LIKE TO LEAVE?

HOW DO YOU SEE THE FUTURE YOU?

THREE

UNCONFORM

IF YOU WANT TO STAND OUT, doing things the same way that 'everyone' else is doing them isn't going to work for you. In fact, doing what everyone else is doing will only make you blend in. Argh!

It's time to *unconform*; to dispense with the same–same 'pastel and marble' way of doing things. It's time to embrace boldness, individuality, creativity and your version of genius. So far, you've done so much in your life – learned and experienced so many things – that you have become quite the individual. Now it's time to showcase this.

Usually, at this point, people tell me they're really not that different to everyone else in their industry. That is the furthest thing from the truth. People tell me that they don't have enough experience; they don't know enough; they're boring (gasp!).

You are the opposite of boring.

The thoughts that have been rolling around in your head are a classic case of the 'devil and angel' sitting on your shoulder. I want you to brace yourself, take a big, deep breath in and as you exhale, I want you to imagine that all of your insecurities and self-doubt are expelled with your breath.

Feels good, doesn't it? Ahhhhh.

You have to acknowledge that these thoughts exist, though, otherwise they don't go away. But you are going to draw a line in the sand right now and declare: *'Not today! I will not let these thoughts rule me today or into the future'*.

DO THE WORK YOU LOVE

I remember a few years ago, I really wanted to transition into doing what I was passionate about. I loved teaching how to create content, how to connect with your audiences and how to own 'brand you' in today's world of social media. I loved helping people to see the potential in themselves that I saw.

> **The world is your oyster. You can create a business around you that you love, doing the work you love and with the people you love.**

The transition for me to doing the work I love was bumpy. I was so afraid that 'the market' (my audience) would be confused. I was totally caught up in thinking that there were other people out there doing it better than I could ever possibly do it. I was advised to *'keep playing my hit song'* because this was the more secure option, and I was afraid of losing money during the transition period. So, I kept going. I allowed the *fear* to win. The fear of it not working. The fear of people not responding. The fear of losing money. The fear of transitioning into the unknown. There was so much fear – and for a while, it won.

At the start of 2018 (not that long ago) I drew a metaphorical line in the sand. I loudly declared, in my office, to anyone who could hear me: *'This is it! I'm done with doing things the way I have been doing them. If it's not fun, I'm not f*cking doing it. If it's not filled with value for others, I'm not f&cking doing it! Come on, Universe! If this is what I'm supposed to be doing, you've now got to do your bit. I'll take all the action in the world, but you've got to play your part. Okay? Okay?'*

With that declaration, I let go of the way I was doing things. I let go of fear. I let go of worrying what anyone else thought about what I was doing or what I wasn't doing. I figured if I 'lost it all' – everything that I'd worked so hard for – then so be it. I was done playing along and 'singing my hit song'. I knew I really had to step into owning my purpose. I needed to work with people I'm passionate about, in a way I'm passionate about. All I wanted to do every single day was to help people, by using my zone of genius. I wanted to have fun, to laugh, to have such amazing clients that we became friends – as well as creating epic freaking results together. The worst thing that could have happened was that my fears would come true. (They didn't.)

FACE YOUR FEAR AND DO IT YOUR WAY ANYWAY

Now we have that out of the way, it's time to step into the rock star version of you! You know what you have inside; let's unleash it to the world. It's time to treat social media as if it's *your own* network. Think of Oprah. She publishes and produces what she wants, knowing that there are people out there who will watch and some who won't.

This is the advice I give to literally every client I work with, regardless of the number of years and qualifications they may have. Every single person I have spoken to over the years knows that they need to increase their visibility and therefore their confidence in the way that they show up.

My clients tell me they want to be more consistent with their message. They tell me they want *more*.

In order to stand out, you really need to approach things differently to the masses. Most people on social media try to appeal to 'everyone'. It's a joyless and futile endeavour, because there will always be people who like you and people who don't. If someone you've never met doesn't like you or what you have to say, does it really matter in the scheme of things? Think about this: in five years' time, will you be thinking about that person or this situation? Of course, the answer is *'hell no!'*, which means that you can leap. You can jump and you can shift your approach.

You need to adjust your attitude from *'I don't know enough'* and *'Everyone else is out there screaming at the top of their lungs, how on earth am I going to be heard?'* to *'People are going to tune into my channel and absorb as much of me as they can, so I'd better have some content for them to eat up!'*.

It's time to own it!

Another way to think about this is that you *are* Netflix or pay TV. You are posting different content all the time, and you will customise it to suit the channel you're posting to.

Facebook is the drama channel, where you share what's been going on. Instagram is the food channel: for some reason, people love seeing what you eat, how you eat and what you're wearing while you're eating over on Instagram! You'll need to approach this channel a little differently.

LinkedIn is the news channel (it's a little dry). Sorry (not sorry). People like reading articles on this channel, but they like to get in and out as quickly as they can – usually in under 10 minutes.

Don't worry, I'll teach you how to work with these platforms later in the book.

When you shift your thinking, the most amazing things happen:

► You realise that you can post on these channels *as much as you damn well please* because you are in control.

► You don't have to worry about what anyone else is doing (or not doing) because you're just doing your thing on your channel.

► You can focus on the value that you bring, rather than worry about what others are saying or doing.

► When you can *focus* on what you're doing (to the exclusion of all else) it empowers you to communicate more, own your authority more and therefore help your audience more.

So many people get caught up with their hopes and dreams of creating a business that affords them the lifestyle, choice and money that they want, but they remain stuck for fear of other people reacting to them adversely. Or, even worse, they fear that nobody is going to listen to them at all.

Think about the band Queen; they were focused on doing what they did best: writing their own music and playing it to the people who wanted to hear it. People could either choose to listen to them or turn them off.

When fear creeps up on you, I advise you to do my 'repattern your fear' activity.

✳ ACTIVITY: Repattern your fear

- Draw two columns on a piece of blank paper.

- Write out each of the fears you have and the things you worry about in the left-hand column. Get them all out of your head.

- On the right-hand side of the page, write why they are total bullshit. It's okay if you repeat reasons.

- Remember that the things we fear rarely come true. They are like the monsters we were afraid of in the night when we were children: they will go away when we wake up to them.

- Shine the light on your fears and doubts and allow yourself to be set free from them.

Think of yourself like a rock star – because, my friend, you are!

I can guarantee you this: most people are afraid to show up and put themselves out there. This gives *you* the perfect opening. You've got the most amazing opportunity available to you right now.

You are going to choose something different to the others. You are going to throw yourself out there – not fearlessly (although some of you will), but in spite of the fear. I love the book *The Alchemist* by Paulo Coelho. In it he writes, *'When you want something, all the universe conspires in helping you to achieve it'*.

When you choose to face your fear and do it anyway, the whole world opens up to you. The audience you want to work with, inspire and motivate, will in fact *love you*. You're going to create content for social media in a way that's aligned with *you*, the things *you're* passionate about and the things *you* stand for.

You will be *unconforming*. You'll find your own way, not the way that 'they' tell you to do things.

Before we move on to taking action, I want to leave you with one more piece of advice:

If it's not fun for you, don't do it.

Draw your line in the sand and declare that you're going to show up, *in the spotlight*, in *your* way, sharing things in the way that aligns with you.

What's the worst thing that could happen? Maybe it doesn't work out. That's okay! You'll have learned some more. You'll have more experience, so you'll be able to pivot and change and try something else.

The best-case scenario is that you'll kick ass. And we know each other well enough by now to know that this is the most likely outcome.

You've got this.

Fear and action cannot exist in the same space. The thing that you're afraid of will dissipate when you start actively doing something in spite of it.

CHAPTER SUMMARY

YOU ARE NOT BORING. EMBRACE YOUR INNER ROCK STAR – YOUR INDIVIDUALITY.

DO THE WORK YOU LOVE.

TREAT SOCIAL MEDIA LIKE YOUR OWN PAY TV.

FACE YOUR FEAR AND KEEP GOING IN SPITE OF IT.

FOUR

TIME TO GET OUT OF THE SHOWER

AFTER READING THIS FAR, you know *why* you need to get into the spotlight.

Now, you need to learn to use the tools and systems that are available to you. The good news is, more often than not they are free! We have never had such comprehensive access to powerful, free, value-based marketing ever. Never. Ever.

We're going to get stuck into the nitty-gritty of using these amazing tools and resources – without it taking 25 hours a day, 8 days per week. We're all busy and most people don't want to spend all day every day on social media creating content.

We're going to go deep as we prepare you to step into the spotlight – *your* spotlight! We do this by exploring four concepts:

1. **Building confidence.** This is where you go from feeling as if all you're doing is singing in the shower – with the four walls as your very fabulous audience – to feeling ready to get out there. You'll be confident it's time to take on the online world.

2. **Finding your hot coal clients.** You're going to explore exactly who you want to have in your audience because, ultimately, they are the people who are going to become your clients. There is a misconception, on social media, that you need to appeal to all and sundry when, in fact, the opposite is true. We are going to get very specific about who this person is that you can bring into your world.

3. **Becoming a rock star.** Most people want to jump straight to this section of the book, because this is where the fun begins. In this part of the book (chapter 6), we explore the energy that you need to shine in the online world. We are going to look at the various platforms that you can show up on and, most importantly, what you're going to do to be seen on those platforms.

   It's crucial you don't jump straight to this chapter because, if you do that, you're not going to build the solid foundation that your personal brand requires to make it sustainable. If you do this part right, your work will see you through for at least the next two years.

4. **Use your influence to become iconic.** Confidence is a natural consequence for people who work through the first three stages. They are confident because they are attracting the 'right' audience, they are truly owning the show and being the rock star they were born to be. Now, it's time to step it up again and use the influence that you have created to become iconic. This is when you can start to influence for even more amazing things.

If you use this process, you'll be able to stand out and be seen. You'll always have unique content and you'll be 'on message' every time.

Why? Because you're about to pull your brilliance out of your head and use it online. You're going to see your amazingness on paper, right in front of you, and you won't be able to deny it a moment longer!

How? Well, I'm going to help you pull it out of your head.

What are you waiting for? Let's roll!

FINDING YOUR INNER CONFIDENCE

I grew up in what felt like the middle of nowhere (which is kind of funny now that I really do live in the middle of nowhere). Our rural block of land backed onto farm land. The crops over our back fence were green and vegetable-like. I'm not sure what they were! The paddocks were huge and sprinklers spanned them, rolling along in one, long line. The water from the sprinklers would form rainbows when the light hit it just 'right'. It was beautiful. One of my favourite things to do was to go to the back of our block and stand on one of the four big, wooden fence posts. I liked the one in the back right-hand corner best, because it gave me the best view, and I was hidden from my brother and my parents! I'd stand up on that fence post and sing my heart out to the crops. I'd wave my arms like a conductor as the plants bent and swayed in the breeze. I remember the faint feeling of mist when the sprinkler-water would get caught up in the breeze and imagined it was my very own fog machine.

At these times, I felt as if I could be anything, do anything. I dreamed that one day I would be a performer, an enter-tainer on television or a famous singer or dancer. There was nothing and nobody to tell me that I couldn't be that person when I 'grew up'. I believed it because I was living it out in my imagination.

Somewhere along the way, though, I lost that inner belief that I could 'make it' doing something like that. I started to believe in the story that society was telling me: I should get a 'proper' job and a 'proper' qualification. I continued to yearn to perform as I got older, but I suppressed this desire. I didn't feel I was good enough; I didn't have the knowledge and skills to pursue a career in the performance industry. Admittedly, at the time, everything was so much less accessible than it is today. My only options were to go to the National Institute of Dramatic Art (NIDA) – and there was no way I would have achieved the marks to get in there. Also, to be honest, I hated learning lines and reciting things that someone else had written!

I didn't feel I had a good enough voice to sing, so becoming a singer was off the table. And dancing? Well, when I was about 10 years old, a ballet teacher told me, *'Your bottom is too big and your back too swayed to ever make it'.* I was heartbroken.

So being an actress – pretending to be someone else – was out; being a singer was out; being a dancer was out. At around 12 or 13 years old I convinced my parents to help me become an Avon lady, dropping cosmetics catalogues. By 16, I was working in a sports store as well as one of the retail shops my parents owned at the time. When I was 19, I went into banking before starting my own business.

I was 'lucky', I guess, compared to many kids. My parents backed all my choices and decisions. If I wanted to pursue something more creative, they would have said 'okay'. If I wanted to be a botanist, they'd have said 'okay'. It didn't matter what I said I wanted to do; I knew they had my back. But I didn't choose to go down the traditional 'creative' pathway. I chose safe.

It took a lot of guts and determination to leave my very secure 12-year corporate (and high-paying) career to embark on starting my own business. I had no safety net, no guarantees... just a whole lot of passion and excitement for helping people be the best versions of themselves and achieve what they want.

For me, even when I was being 'professional' and working in a 'proper' job, the yearning to be more, do more and create something more powerful was still there – it would come out at different times when my guard was down. It was a little bit like how I imagined Freddie Mercury felt in the film *Bohemian Rhapsody* when he was standing in the crowd, thinking, *'That should be me up there'*.

We learn in the movie that Freddie's father pushed him to get a 'real' job. Thank God he had the inner confidence to follow his dreams.

The risk that you run, if you don't find the inner confidence to move forward and chase your dreams, is that you'll be stuck forever singing to the crops or the four walls of the shower. You'll be the world's best-kept secret.

IT'S ALL ABOUT MINDSET

Stepping into the spotlight is an ongoing mindset game. At every new level you reach in your business, your mindset will need to go up a gear to push you to a new, fabulous level. It can be uncomfortable, but we all know that magic is created when we're outside of our comfort zones.

The key is to create a way to hone your confidence and become unstoppable. Remember, you know more than you give yourself credit for. You are an expert at what you do, the way you do it and who you do it with.

I think you know me well enough by now to realise there's going to be some tough love in this book. I'm not going to paint you some magical picture of unicorns who fart glitter, or lull you into believing that there's a freaking magic pill. There's not. But the things I will share with you work. I've been using all them literally all day, every day since 2010. I've been teaching other business owners how to do this since 2011.

I believe in you and I know you can do this.

The risks of not embracing the spotlight are huge and will have an adverse impact on your visibility. Here is what could happen if you don't develop the right mindset to push yourself out of your comfort zone:

- Nobody is going to see you and you'll continue to be invisible to the people you want to help. (Ouch.)

- You'll forever be a dreamer; a wanna-be-er; an I-would-love-to-do-this-prenuer who never gets anywhere.

- Self-sabotage will reign supreme. This is where the dreaded devil and angel who live on your shoulders will fight, and the devil will always win.

- Fear will keep you stuck.

- Your business will flounder.

- To add salt to the wound, you'll see your competitors get themselves out there and thrive.

- Your confidence will go through the floor and you'll make the decision that being in business just isn't for you; that you didn't really want to do it anyway.

- You'll forever be like Freddie at the start of *Bohemian Rhapsody*, looking wistfully up at the people who are up on stage, living their dreams.

We all take for granted the things that we do so freaking well; those things that happen almost without us having to think about them too much. It could be the way you coach or train people, the way you operate your business, or your wonderful ability to always know the exact right thing to say when someone asks you for help and advice.

You need to acknowledge that these things that you do almost unconsciously are actually clues to your zone of awesomeness, which is going to support your efforts to get into the spotlight.

You don't want to get to the end of your life regretting the chances you didn't take. You don't want to lament not making the impact that you wanted, wishing for your time over again, knowing that it's an impossibility.

The time is now, my friend. I know you can do this.

A healthy mindset underpins your entire success. With an unhealthy mindset, you'll be subject to the roller-coaster of day-to-day emotions.

There are four components to cultivating a great mindset, which in turn leads you to feel more confident to get your ideas, your thoughts and your gorgeous face out into the world. The components are:

1. Resilience

2. Goals

3. Strengths

4. Knowledge.

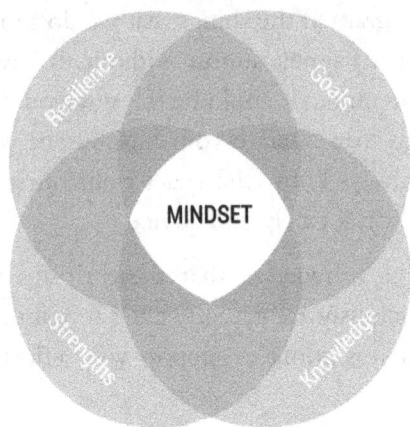

Let's expand on each in the following sections.

Resilience

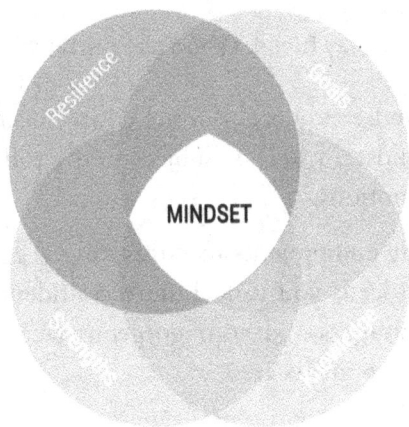

Resilience is defined as *'the capacity to recover quickly from dif-ficulties; toughness'*.

In her documentary *Miss Americana*, Taylor Swift says, *'When you're living for the approval of strangers, and that is where you derive all of your joy and fulfillment, one bad thing can cause every-thing to crumble'.* So many business owners rely on external validation to remind themselves how excellent and amazing they are. The problem is that, sometimes, one negative comment can make everything go downhill fast.

The hardest part of business, and growing your visibility, is working on your mindset and ensuring that you have some strategies in place to protect yourself from external and internal triggers that impact you.

Here are some common mindset-related issues that will test your resilience:

- Fear of failure
- Wondering if anyone will even listen when you put yourself out there
- Imposter syndrome (groan! This one's a doozy)
- The fear of not being good enough
- The fear of not belonging
- The fear of not being loved by 'the people'
- Worrying about how much time something is going to take
- Procrastination on doing what you need to do
- Worrying about perceived negative feedback.

According to commonly referenced statistics, 95 per cent of businesses fail within the first five years, and a lot of those failures could have been avoided if the business owners had addressed their mindset. Why? Because if you have a healthy mindset, you are a healthy problem-solver. You are resourceful, resilient and will seek people to help you. If you have the mindset to learn all you can, you'll be fine. If you learn *how* to manage cash flow, you'll make informed decisions. If you learn all you can about marketing and sales, you'll always be able to land on your feet.

You are going to cultivate the most powerful internal resilience so that you no longer have to rely on the external approval of others to validate you and remind you that you deserve your spotlight. Building your visibility (and your business) comes with its own unique set of challenges that anyone outside of that world just doesn't understand.

Resilience is an important topic, because so many people think that businesses are built overnight and are super-successful instantly (thanks internet!). The reality is that for every 'overnight success' we hear about, there are often years that have gone before the success hits.

Angela Duckworth, author of *Grit*, writes, *'Nobody wants to show you the hours and hours of becoming. They'd rather show the highlight of what they've become.'*

It's common to hide behind the glitz, glamour and accolades and allow everyone to think that you're perfect and that everything's easy. But the reality is that there are so many failures, stressors and tough situations that you need to get through before you achieve success.

You need to accept this. It's part of developing a healthy mindset, and that is what is going to see you through to becoming iconic. You'll be able to use your success and your influence to propel your legacy and your mission in this world.

Embrace failure

Here's what you need to do. You need to embrace the fact that you're going to fail – a lot. You'll start putting yourself out there and people won't seem to respond. You'll put out sales campaigns that generate no revenue or won't hit the targets. You'll find people copy you – unashamedly – sometimes even word for word! (Yes, it happens. Plagiarism still exists on the internet, but there are some who think that it's a free for all.) You'll probably look silly sometimes. You'll do some things where your hair isn't right or you'll have lipstick on your teeth; technology won't always play along.

You can't control any of that. When these things happen, you have two choices:

1. You can choose to let anything and everything derail you; or

2. You can take it on the chin and remind yourself that there is no failure, only learning; that you choose to be the most resilient person out there who is going to keep getting knocked down and getting up again.

Many years ago, I remember a mentor sharing with me that the successful people are those who are too stupid to stay lying on the ground when they get knocked down. They keep getting up. I couldn't agree more.

Chinese proverb: Fall down seven times, get up eight.

Nobody is immune to things going awry. No matter what you do, no matter how tightly you try to control everything and manage everything, sometimes shit happens.

I remember in 2017, I had a group of women going through a training program that I'd been running since 2012. I ran it live. Out of the six women who went through that program, three of them didn't do 'the work'. (They even told me on a live training call that was recorded that they hadn't done the work!) They decided to blame me at the end of the training, saying it was 'too much work' and demanded their money back. Naturally, I said 'no', so they threatened a class action. They threatened to take me to the media and drag my family through the drama-fuelled current affairs programs and defame me over social media.

I held my ground. But when it was over, I was shell-shocked and heartbroken. I had been running my business for seven years; I'd had hundreds of clients who had been through my training and consulting. Logically, I knew it wasn't my fault. Emotionally, I was devastated. It took a while to come back from that experience, because it made me question everything.

I kept reminding myself at the time that: *'I can only control me. I know that I have done the right thing. This experience is helping me to be more resilient and to help others who may experience a similar situation'.*

It doesn't matter what you do; even if you do *everything* 'right', humans are humans. You can, however, control how you respond and react.

> **Side note: What experiences have you been through that have helped you to grow and build resilience?**

Nothing is ever as bad as we make it out in our heads to be.

Brené Brown in *Rising Strong* talks about when you're writing your shitty first draft (often in your own head), the things that you're talking about, thinking about and agonising over have been blown out of proportion and are not necessarily founded in reality. Saying things like, *'Everyone hates me'* or, *'Nobody is going to buy my product'* is a knee-jerk reaction to protect yourself from feeling ashamed by your situation. You need to air it in the open, embrace your fear, talk about it with a loved one, your coach or mentor, and let them know what you're deeply afraid of and why. This is a call for vulnerability, and it will serve you for your entire life and throughout your journey into the spotlight and beyond.

Step up with courage

I urge you to step up with courage. It can feel as if there are haters and trolls on the internet, just waiting for your content to go up so they can pull it apart, pull *you* apart, and rip you to shreds. It's normal to worry about negative feedback, so don't be alarmed. However, you can't let it thwart your efforts or hold you back.

I worried for a really long time about people judging me. I worried that they would laugh at me behind my back – or, worse, to my face – until I learned this phrase in 2010: *'It's not my business what anyone else thinks of me'*. It was then that I looked at the facts:

- ► Humans judge each other every minute of every day – more so these days because of the internet. You have to form opinions in milliseconds about what content you're going to allow past the gatekeeper to grab your attention, so you judge constantly. Anyone who says they don't, quite frankly, is not human.

➤ You may well cop some flack when you start really throwing yourself out there, and that's okay, but you have to let it wash off you like water off a duck's back.

You cannot, even for a moment, let criticism – real or anticipated – hold you back from getting yourself out there. Every single person has an opinion and every single person is perfectly entitled to that opinion. However, if you're letting their opinion derail you, you'll need to recalibrate and find the courage to keep moving forward.

Some opinions will sting more than others; for example, comments made by friends and family. Yes! The people who you know love you and care about you often make the comments that most need to be censored!

When you're preparing to launch yourself out into the stratosphere so you can create the business and life you want and deserve, it's natural to talk about what you're doing and how you're doing to do it with those you love and care about. However, be prepared, my friend. They may not understand what you're doing and they might not be as encouraging as you'd like them to be. Why? Because they feel it's their duty to protect you and to keep you 'safe'. You are likely to hear stories from them about people they know who failed or whose business didn't work. Or someone who looked like a dill because they did something differently. They may even tell you that they can't see *how* you can make this work 'in this day and age'.

They may not see it but *you can!*

You need to be super-cautious about whose voice you let inside your brain.

I remember when I was starting out with my business in 2010. I was at the point where I was keen for all the encouragement possible. I was talking to people about what I was doing, and they didn't understand how I could build a business from the middle of nowhere, working with people around the world. They asked:

'How are you going to make money?'

'How are you going to find clients?'

'What if it doesn't work? Will you go back and get a job?'

These questions seem innocent enough, but if your confidence is at the lower end of the scale, they can derail you.

The best possible piece of advice I can give you or anyone else in this position is to *not* tell people what you're doing! Be discerning about what you share and with whom. When people ask me how things are going, I say, *'Things are great, thanks! What about you?'* It doesn't matter if I'm in the middle of the worst month ever, or the best month ever. I only speak openly with people who I know will be encouraging and supportive of what I'm doing.

Sometimes you can't avoid people saying stupid shit to you! (There's really no other way of saying it.) Some people just don't think about what's coming out of their mouths – they have no filter. Don't take it personally, just get back to work. You've got this.

You've got to be resilient and call on your inner grit to keep going. The old saying *'what doesn't kill you, makes you stronger'* is certainly right. It's important to acknowledge that there are ebbs and flows and sometimes your mindset is going to be in the toilet and other times you'll be flying high.

Remember, the stories you're telling yourself in your head are really just shitty first drafts. They don't hold any control over you.

We all have fears and worries and concerns when it comes to stepping up and out of our comfort zones. You're not alone. You're amazing. You've got this.

Let's take a look at what else you can do to bolster your confidence to get your butt out of the shower and into the spotlight.

GOALS

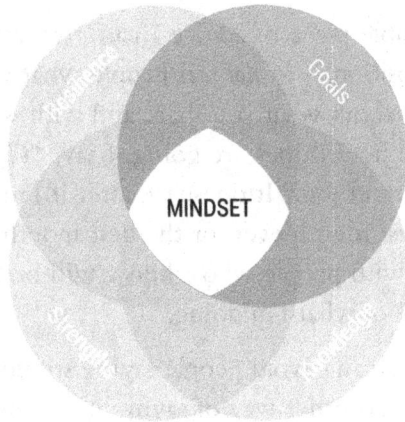

In his book *Relentless*, Tim Grover writes about the training regime of famous athletes such as Kobe Bryant and Michael Jordan, and what they do to stay on top of their game and achieve their goals. For some, it's about being the best; winning championships with their team. Early on in the book, he shares something that I love: *'I'm telling you to crave the result so intensely that the work is irrelevant'.*

It's crucial that you are aligned with your goals and that you know what you want and why.

I have a different approach to goals to many other 'visibility experts'. Being visible online isn't about just being visible. Being 'an influencer' – where you get free stuff to promote (that's *not* what this book is about by any stretch of the imagination) – is not a goal.

For some people, their goals revolve around money, because money enables them to have choice and freedom for themselves and for their families. For others, it's about creating a business that they can sell or franchise. For others still, it's about leaving a legacy.

Whatever your goals are, they are *your* goals and that's awesome.

What do you want to achieve specifically over the next three years? If you try to look further ahead than that, your goals can feel unachievable. Once you're clear on your three-year goals, what do you need to do over the next 12 months to make inroads towards those goals? Then, what do you specifically need to do over the next 90 days, and the next 30?

It's awesome to set goals, but the problem I've found for both myself and for my clients is that when they are so big and feel so far away, it can be tough to keep them top of mind. If they feel unachievable, it's hard to be motivated by them.

I first started reverse-engineering my goals in 2011 and I've been using this strategy ever since to stay on track.

Michael Jordan is very famous for saying, *I've missed more than 9,000 shots in my career. I've lost almost 300 games. Twenty-six times, I've been trusted to take the game-winning shot and missed. I've failed over and over and over again in my life'.* The only reason he kept showing up and kept trying was because his goals were more important than his failures. He effectively reverse-engineered his goals by making sure he was the person who practised harder than anyone else, trained harder than anyone else and was willing to fail more than anyone else.

✳ ACTIVITY: What are your goals?

Take some time to think about what you'd like to achieve in these areas of your life. Write your goals down in the space provided.

Health ....

....

Love ....

....

Social life ....

....

Fun ....

....

For your soul ....

....

STRENGTHS

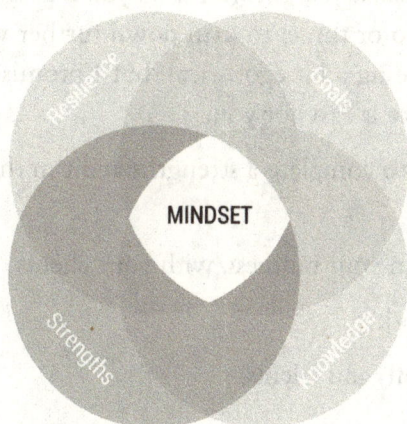

We're going to have some fun with this one, okay? You have more going for you than you've ever given yourself credit for, my friend! The most interesting thing that I find when I'm discussing this topic with people is that the things that are very clearly their strengths are the same things they tend to take for granted or downplay.

For instance, I have a client who speaks in the most calm and soothing way; she puts everyone at ease when she's talking about the things she's passionate about. (I have calm-envy! I'm naturally exuberant and bubbly – I've rarely been described as 'calming'!) When I pointed out to her that this was how others felt around her, she seemed genuinely surprised and delighted. It was something she hadn't really considered before, because she took it for granted. She hadn't realised that one of her superpowers was just being herself.

People have myriad strengths. If I were to ask you right now, *'What do you think your strengths are?'* you'd probably only be able to list two or three; to drill down further would feel as if you were being a bit egotistical, but I promise you you're not. Let's make it easy for you.

You're going to complete a strengths audit in three different areas:

1. At work/in your business/with your clients

2. Not at work

3. Natural gifts and talents.

Ask people at work what they think are your *top three strengths* – the things that they regard as your biggest assets. (Make sure you ask them to name only positive ones!) Don't prompt them, let them come up with their own words. Be sure to tell them that you are super-grateful to them for sharing. When I've done this, I've framed my request like this: *'I'm going to ask you for some help and it makes me vomit a little, but here goes! What do you think are my three biggest strengths?'*.

Next, ask the same question of people who are not at work – your family or people you play sport or share hobbies with. People you hang out with regularly are good people to ask.

When it comes to your natural gifts and talents, I want you to sit and brainstorm everything and anything that people have told you that you are good or great at, which may have made you scratch your head! It could be that people have said, *'You always know the exact right thing to say'*, or *'I know I can always count on you to help me out'*, or *'You have the gift of the gab!*

I couldn't do what you do'. We don't often acknowledge our natural gifts and talents. However, they are super-important to keep front of mind because, when you're having a bad day, reminding yourself that you have them can boost your confidence.

Psychologist Martin Seligman, author of *Authentic Happiness*, created a 'strengths survey' that you can access online (for free) to find out what your top natural strengths are. The good news is, when you learn these, you can further draw on them when you're under pressure or even when you're stepping into something new. Like now! (Head to www. authentichappiness.org. Choose the VIA survey of character strengths. There are 250 questions, so make sure you set some time aside. You'll get a result at the end of the survey to show you what your natural strengths are.)

Completing this survey helped me to realise that my 'zest, enthusiasm and energy' for life are things that I can draw on daily and use to inspire and motivate others. Knowing this has helped me because, whenever I need to step up and out into something uncomfortable or unfamiliar, I can tap into these strengths. It's also made me realise that it's more than okay for me to be me and appreciate that not everyone has these top strengths. You've got to use what you've got, my friend!

KNOWLEDGE

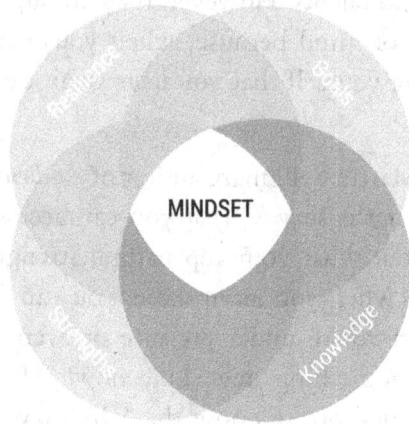

Raise your hand if you've ever been struck by imposter syndrome. We touched on it earlier. It's the type of thing that can knock you off kilter and have you throwing your hands in the air in a tantrum, declaring to the world, *'Everyone knows more than I do. I don't know enough. Maybe I should go and do some more study'.* (Never mind the extensive studying you've likely already done, the experience you have the myriad certifications, online courses and workshops you've been to or the books you've read.)

You already know enough to step into the spotlight!

You have the most amazing amount of experience and knowledge that you don't give yourself credit for. You've probably been working since you were 15 or 16 years old – if not earlier. You've done some kind of study or learning over the past five years (even if it's listening to podcast after podcast about an area that you want to learn more about).

The trap many business owners fall into is believing that they have to have 2,343,984 degrees before they can get themselves out there; or 'x' number of hours of experience before they can do this. It's total bullshit.

You know more than your audience knows and you know how to help them! That makes you an expert in their eyes. It's time to start owning that.

Here are some practical things you can do to see how freakishly amazing you are:

- Do an audit of your formal learning experiences in five-year blocks from when you were 15 years old. What were you studying/doing from age 15 to 20, 20 to 25 and so on?

- Complete an audit of your informal learning experiences in the same manner. If you did a first aid course, if you've had personal development training, if you went on a corporate 'retreat' where you learned about personality types, you learned stuff – so document it. (Note, this doesn't mean you're going to educate other people in these areas, it just highlights to you that you've completed more learning and have more experiences than you give yourself credit for.)

- What are your opinions about your industry and why do you hold them? What pisses you off about your industry, so much that you want to get up on your soapbox and rant about it? What evidence do you have to support this? What experiences have you had that have caused you to think like this?

➤ What do you love about your industry, so much so that you would shout it from the heavens for all and sundry to hear? What evidence do you have to support this? What experiences have caused you to think like this?

➤ What personalised process do you take your clients through and why do you think this is a great thing to do? If you've been working with people for more than six months, you've probably found and created nuances within what you do. What are they?

NOW YOU'RE OUT OF THE SHOWER!

You now have a very practical and simple way to bolster and grow your confidence. You can see that there are so many parts to you that are completely awesome, which will help you step into the spotlight. (Don't worry, I'll share with you *how* to do this in upcoming chapters.)

Using these strategies, you'll feel inspired to take the next steps, because you'll start to see that you are unique. Nobody else has the same fingerprint as you, the same opinions as you or the same way of backing them up as you. Why? Because you are unique and brilliant.

Far too often I hear that people think there are too many people in their industry, so they're not going to be able to stand out. Part of the reason that this prophecy becomes true is because they're scared to death of looking different, because they haven't got the bedrock of confidence to support them.

You have this foundation in place now. You can see the evidence from both an internal perspective and an external perspective. You've got goals. You know what you need to do to achieve them. And now you have the confidence to chase after them.

You're also armed with a fresh dose of reality that you're likely going to fail at some point. It's true. You are. I've failed countless times. I've tried to sell training that nobody has bought. I've launched offers and all I've heard is crickets. I've also launched programs that have achieved tens of thousands of dollars in sales. Why? Because from everything that hasn't worked, I've learned something, so I was able to pivot and adjust until it did work.

You now have the confidence to do the same thing.

**You're not singing in the shower anymore, baby!
Time for the world to hear that wonderful voice of yours.**

Remember earlier when I was telling you about my singing to the crops? I loved the physical feeling when I was doing that. I felt fearless, weightless and free. I felt confident, funny, fun and like an entertainer with that childlike abandon that I'm sure you remember feeling at some point.

We need to get back to that, not worrying so much about having the perfect voice, the perfect tone, the perfect outfit, the perfect experience, the perfect childhood, the perfect education. Pretend you're me, but your version of me, singing to that huge audience of crops. That's how you're going to feel when we get you into the spotlight.

Confident.

Certain.

Powerful.

Free to be YOU.

INTERVIEW WITH ADAM THOMPSON, FROM CHOCOLATE STARFISH

It's important to find a way of expressing ourselves emotionally – and it takes confidence to do that. Adam uses music, which is a big reason why he got into music in the first place. He shared with me that he would experiment with his voice, using two tape recorders (yes, a machine that played cassette tapes – remember those?). He'd have one tape playing music and use the other to record himself singing, so he could hear what he sounded like.

He recalls seeing an ad in the paper for a singer. He thought it would be for a wedding or another event, but instead, he found that it was placed by a piano player on the lookout for a singer. He answered the ad and they spent some time writing a song together. This sparked the realisation in Adam that he could use music as a vehicle for expressing himself.

When it comes to confidence and performing, he says, *'I can perform and I can do it with 100 per cent confidence and 100 per cent belief'.*

That's what it takes for you to be able to show up in the way that I'm encouraging you to. You've got to find any way possible to be able to back yourself and be 100 per cent authentic in those moments.

To read/hear the full interview, make sure you head to www.nicolamoras.com.au/intothespotlight

CHAPTER SUMMARY

WHAT HAVE YOU BEEN THROUGH THAT'S HELPED YOU GROW YOUR RESILIENCE?

WHAT ARE YOUR GOALS IN VARIOUS AREAS OF YOUR LIFE?

DO A STRENGTHS AUDIT TO FIND OUT FROM OTHERS WHAT THEY THINK YOUR STRENGTHS ARE.

COMPLETE A KNOWLEDGE AUDIT TO BOOST YOUR CONFIDENCE.

FIVE
HOT COAL CLIENTS™

THE SUN WAS BEATING DOWN on his head as he sang and played his keyboard in the middle of the day. He was positioned in the centre of the mall to maximise the number of people passing by. Most would avoid eye contact and walked on, until there was a song that he played that someone loved. It stopped them in their tracks, and they'd stand watching, tapping their feet. They'd feel around in their pockets for coins (never notes) and sometimes they'd throw some money in the hat to encourage him.

What the people passing by didn't understand was how much heart and soul this man put into his music. He played and played, sang and sang as if music were his oxygen. Some of the songs he played accurately conveyed this and others not so much.

This man has been playing for years and, in order to make money, he would primarily sing covers of other artists – from Queen to INXS to The Angels to AC/DC to James Blunt to Guns N' Roses. He knew certain songs would stop people in their tracks and he'd make money.

But he really wanted to play his own music. He'd throw some of his own work into the playlist most times he busked, but the truth of the matter was that people seemed to be unwilling to stop, listen and then give him money when he played his own songs.

The same thing happened when he was playing at pubs and other gigs. The agreement with the bars was that he would play songs the crowd knew, because it got them drinking more, laughing more and dancing more, which meant that they spent more money. Yes, bars are businesses too, you know! The more drinks that get spilled from drinking and dancing, the more money gets taken over the bar. It makes complete sense when it's spelled out like that, doesn't it?

Our muso's creativity was being stifled. He was constantly at the mercy of whatever the bar wanted him to do, which would depend on the crowd that night. Wednesday's crowd was more easy listening and Friday's was more classic rock. *'Play to the crowd'*, they'd say. And he did. Until it all got too much. There was so much more that he wanted to play, different music he wanted to bring to the world. He was desperately hoping for his big break, but it just never seemed to come. He was beginning to think it probably never would, if all he did was continue to play other people's music in other people's venues.

He'd been doing 'the work' in the time when he wasn't performing, sending demos to music producers, trying to build networks and connections, publishing original music on the internet, looking for any way to get his own music out there.

But he knew he had to do something different otherwise this was going to be as good as it would get.

You can easily become pigeonholed if you are only marketing in a very general way, and always pivoting and adjusting from audience to audience, platform to platform.

I'm going to talk about how to build your audience a little later in this book but, for the meantime, I need you to decide – no, I need you to *declare* – that you're going to create your own audience. You are going to create your own 'pub' so that you can play to the audience you want to and play the songs you want to – your originals – and have people love them and you.

You do your best and most powerful work when you're working with people you actually *like*. You know this to be true. They are the people you would almost literally walk over hot coals for and do close to anything for. These are what I call hot coal clients. They are the people we want in our audience.

YOU NEED TO FIND YOUR AUDIENCE

Far too often, we get caught up with the face that stares back at us in the mirror every morning, rather than thinking about our audience. It's really normal to worry that you're not going to get it right, that things aren't going to land with your audience the way you wanted them to. It's normal to fear the repercussions of putting yourself out there, which could range anywhere from zero repercussions (as in nobody at all even sees or hears you) right through to there being many repercussions as you start to build the right audience.

We are all weirdos! Most of us feel as if we don't fit in. We're odd, weird, different and strange. Let's face it, entrepreneurs particularly are a funny bunch of humans! I've spent the majority of my life feeling as if I don't fit in with most people I know.

What you need to do is get out of your own way and accept that this 'stepping into the spotlight' gig isn't actually about you at all. It's about finding a way to help your audience feel like they belong somewhere, like they fit with you. They want to feel that you understand them (not the other way around).

To do this, you need to learn *how* to communicate with your audience. You need to stop thinking that it's all about you (like it was when you were singing in the shower!) and, instead, move past busking and hoping for the attention of all and sundry, and really start to hone in on exactly who your people are.

Who are your weirdos? Weirdos unite!

This chapter is all about getting into your audience's psyche. You'll learn how to find out more about them and what makes them tick. Then, you'll find ways to connect to and engage with them in a way that helps them learn to trust you – you are *their* weirdo and they are yours!

You're going to get super-clear on your hot coal clients, because this will help *you* to communicate with your audience. It's going to help you connect with them. And this is going to make your content creation easier (don't worry, we'll talk about that in chapter 6).

Every single human on the planet is seeking acceptance and validation – acceptance that they're not *that* weird and validation that their fears, vision and goals are real – and that how they feel doesn't make them a freak of nature. Gosh darn it, they're normal and the more you can get inside their heads, the more you're going to be able to help alleviate all their fears and worries.

So, why do you want to do this? For purely selfish reasons, my friend, because it makes *your* life easier. It also helps you to build *relationships* with people.

BUILDING RELATIONSHIPS

Take a look at the relationship-building process in the image below. This demonstrates the process of building trust.

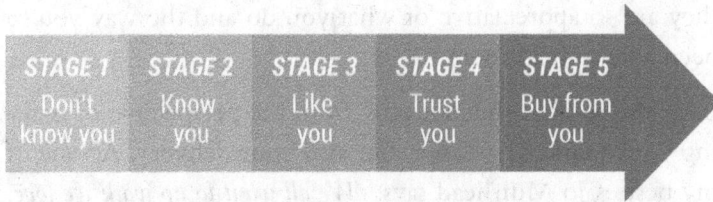

STAGE 1	STAGE 2	STAGE 3	STAGE 4	STAGE 5
Don't know you	Know you	Like you	Trust you	Buy from you

Stage 1. At first people don't even know who you are. They don't know you exist. And then BAM! They see you on the internet and they are curious, because you've stopped them in the middle of whatever they were doing (probably scrolling, scrolling, s-c-r-o-l-l-i-n-g!) and they move to stage 2.

Stage 2. In this phase, people start to get to know you. They're following you online, watching and listening to what you're sharing. You are visible to them, because you're posting and sharing great content. They feel like they're really able to experience you, learn from you and get to know you.

Stage 3. The natural consequence of you showing up online and sharing yourself and your expertise is that people start to *like you!* Shazam! When people feel that you 'get them', understand them and can help them, they will like you more.

Stage 4. Now you are building trust. In his book, *The 7 Habits of Highly Effective People*, Stephen R. Covey talks about adding to the 'trust account', and when you're marketing yourself online, this is what happens. You're out there adding value, helping people, giving hints, tips and pieces of advice.

Stage 5. This is when they buy from you, because you become their trusted adviser. They recommend you and they'll repeat buy from you. They will advocate for you and they are so appreciative of what you do and the way you've been able to help them.

Let's also look at this not only from the perspective of making your marketing easier, but also your delivery. As one of my besties Jo Muirhead says, *'We all want to do work we love, with people we love and the way we love to do'.* Who on earth wants to work with people they don't even like? Not me, that's for sure.

If you do the activities in this chapter, you'll get crystal clear on who these people actually are. It will mean that you're more likely to fill your marketing funnel with people you'll get along with, like to work with and enjoy hanging out with. That's a win–win, right?

When you are super-clear on who these people are, you'll be able to create content that resonates with them, which means you'll *cut through the noise* online. You'll stand out to them. You'll be seen as different to every other man, woman, child and Frenchie on the internet.

Hallelujah! No more yelling to try and be heard. No more trying to convince anyone that they need you. No more feeling as if you're talking to a blank, empty void.

Let's get down to business.

There are three main stages I'm going to walk you through to help you find and work with hot coal clients.

STAGE 1: WHO ARE YOUR HOT COAL CLIENTS?

One of the most powerful things you can do when you're setting yourself up to step into the spotlight is to *imagine* the people you want to work with in your mind's eye. It helps if you can visualise someone amazing who you know you'd love to work with. It could be a visual image of someone you've already worked with who you loved. It could be someone who you had a lot of fun with and also achieved great results with.

Doing this activity below will help.

✳ ACTIVITY: Use your imagination

I want you to imagine yourself in the biggest stadium you can think of. (Football stadiums are often a good place to start with this one.) There's a stage, and you are waiting backstage, getting primped and preened. You look freaking amazing! Hot. Gorgeous. Handsome. Beautiful. Stunning. You're glowing because you know you're about to walk out onto that stage at any minute and 'wow' the crowd with your amazing opera singing. Yes, you are an opera singer and you are amazing at what you do.

You get the cue and out you go to the cheers of the crowd. You scan the stadium and notice that many people in the crowd are wearing black AC/DC t-shirts. This seems kind of weird, but you carry on. You walk up to the microphone, and you start singing.

INTO THE SPOTLIGHT

The crowd has gone quiet and as you look out at the faces in front of you they seem somewhat confused. You see them fumble around with the program and try to work out what's going on. Some are checking their tickets.

People start to exit the stadium in droves, while you're there, giving the performance of your life.

What you didn't know was that the promoters knew that they had to fill the stadium in order to fulfil their contract with you, so they gave away a lot of tickets. They dragged people in off the streets with the promise of a free concert. They told them there would be a 'variety' of music being played that night, and that they'd enjoy it. Some were told that they'd won tickets to AC/DC or Guns N' Roses – the polar opposite to opera!

You don't ever want to have your stadiums filled with people who aren't 'your people'. You want the right audience to show up – the people who love you (and, in this case people who love opera!).

You are responsible for showing up and making sure that your audience is closely aligned to you, your style and your way of doing things, so that when they do buy from you (and they will), they don't feel confused about what they are getting.

How to get to know your audience

It's time now to get to know your audience so that you can fill up your online stadium with as many of these people as you can.

88

First things first. To make it as easy as humanly possible for you to do this, you're going to answer these basic questions:

- Do you want to work primarily with men or women? (Just choose one, because it helps you to get a mental image of someone you'd love to work with.)

- How old are they?

- Are they married or single?

- Do they have children and, if yes, how old are they?

  I feel like I need to share an aside with you here. No, it doesn't really matter what a person's marital status is because I know you can help anyone with what you do. But, people who are married have a different set of circumstances, different stressors and a different reality to those who are single. Just as those who have young children have a very different reality right now to someone whose children have just left home. Trust me. Roll with this; it will make your life easier!

- What do they do for a living?

- If they have a partner, what does their partner do for a living?

- Where do they live?

- What kind of car do they drive?

- What are their goals and dreams?

- What are their stress points?

- What do they really *not* like about their life?

- What is their health like?

- What is their mindset like?

- What is their financial situation? (Hopefully, they're not broke – unless you're operating a charity. You need people to be able to pay you!)

- What keeps them up at night – their worst-case scenario? (And how does this relate to what you do?)

Here's where the activities start. You are going to create a character by summarising the answers to all of the above questions. This will give you a clear outline of the person you want to bring into the business. You'll give this person a name, so that when your eyes are closed, you can think to yourself, *'What does Hailey need to hear today?'* or *'What does Roger need today to take a step forward?'*.

A graphic designer's hot coal client

Name	Theresa
Age and gender	45-year-old woman
What they do for a living	entrepreneur
Relationship status	married
Partner's job	husband is employed FT and earns $150k+ per year. Is sometimes away but not often enough for it to be a problem.
Children	two
Where they live	in the suburbs
Car they drive	a Jeep. Husband has a company car as well.

Goals and dreams

She's been building her business and initially it was a way to bring in a little bit of extra money, but she's since been bitten by the bug – the entrepreneur bug!

She's been getting one-on-one clients and that's going well. She knows she wants to grow, but she doesn't know what she wants that to look like. What she really wants is to 'uplevel' her business. She wants to create a brand that is on point for her; that aligns with her personality and where she's going. She's chatted to a few of her friends and they've all told her that she's nuts! She should *just be happy with what she has'*, but she's not. So, instead of talking with them even more about what she wants to create, she keeps it inside.

Mindset

She's a go-getter; driven, ambitious and hungry to make this business work even better.

Stress points

She has no more hours to sell. She wants to help more clients but there's no time. She's frustrated and tired. Her husband tells her to do whatever it is that she needs to do to change the situation because he wants his happy wife back. The kids are hanging for more attention. She's time-poor and feels guilty for not spending the time they want her to with them. Yet she can't take the foot off the pedal, otherwise everything will implode.

She's done 'everything' and tried 'everything' and searched for 'everyone'. She's been looking for a better way. She knows there must be a better way but can't even imagine the next steps.

She's intuitive about what other people need to hear, so why can't she use her intuition for herself? She just can't seem to tap into the 'thing' that's going to make her business work and take it up a level.

Truthfully, she wants to reinvent herself. She wants to lead with strength. She wants to find the people who really need her and do the things that she does best.

What she really doesn't like about her life

Honestly, our graphic designer is a bit pissed off with it all. She's getting busier and busier and doesn't want to lose the momentum. She's stuck on the carousel of sameness and doesn't know how to break out. She doesn't love how her business is working anymore. She was in love with it initially and now it's feeling like a lot of work. She can't articulate what she wants to create. She can't describe what it is – but she knows there's something missing.

Health

She's not really happy with her health overall. She doesn't really get the time to focus on physical activity. She doesn't exercise anywhere near as much as she should (and wants to). She doesn't take time out for self-care. She eats pretty healthily, but still has days when she can't be bothered and just eats whatever she can get her hands on.

Financial situation

Her business is going well but she wants more. Her husband has a well-paid job, so they don't need to worry about money. But she wants to contribute financially to the household.

She has set a goal to create $500,000 to $1 million per year in revenue and then grow from there. She does have money blocks, though, and feels like she's going around and around in circles.

Her 3 am story

In the wee hours, she's awake worrying about her business and whether it's going to be able to reach the heights that she dreams of. She worries about the time she's sacrificing with her children to grow the business and hopes that it's going to pay off. She worries about her husband sharing her mindset and what happens if he doesn't. She's worries about making more money in her business because her husband has been talking about joining her to work in her business together. What if it all comes crashing down? What if she loses it all?

Uncovering problems

Every one of your hot coal clients will have a problem, or many problems. There will be one specific problem that you can solve for them, as well as a whole cluster of issues in other areas of their lives.

I ask every one of my clients to complete my '54 problem solution' activity, which covers off the nine main areas in every human's life:

1. Health
2. Business/career
3. Soul
4. Family
5. Social
6. Fun
7. Money
8. Mindset
9. Love (relationship).

Your audience is unlikely to rank 10/10 satisfied in all areas of their life, and this exercise will uncover their problems, stress points and challenges in each area. Try this activity for yourself.

✳ ACTIVITY: 54 problem solution

List at least six problems/stressors/challenges in each of the categories given on the previous page. (You'll get to 54 pretty quickly!)

For example:

Health

1. I'm not as strong as I'd like to be

2. I can't make it to the gym

3. I'm not fat but not skinny. I'd be happy to lose 5kg

4. I'm not as fit as I used to be

5. I drink too much coffee. I really should do something about that

6. I need to get up and move more. My posture is crap.

Love

1. My partner and I don't tend to have date nights very often these days

2. Why can't we be the couple that everyone envies?

3. I just don't feel like I'm in love anymore

4. The kids have really taken over all our time. How do we get back to where we were?

5. I have no family support to go on date nights

6. What if my partner is having an affair? Argh!

We're a beautiful mass of contradictions

The beautiful thing about humans is that we're a mass of walking contradictions and your hot coal clients are no different. As the saying goes, there are two sides to every coin.

It's important that you identify all the different facets of your hot coal clients because when you get into the next chapter, when we start marketing to them, you need to find different ways of catching their attention.

For example, some people love camping but also love staying in five-star hotels (I know, it's not just me!). You could capture my attention on social media by sharing a glamping story or photo (come on, you didn't really think I'd be into full-on camping, did you?). Additionally, you could capture my attention with a photo of you staying at the Bellagio in Las Vegas. I love both these things, and I know that your audience has a list as long as their arm of things that they love as well.

Think of your hot coal clients as a disco ball.

THE DISCO BALL!

Each facet represents a different part of them.

✳ ACTIVITY: List the contradictions

For example, your hot coal client is a 45-year-old woman who loves yoga and:

- Loves going out dancing
- Loves meditating
- Loves rocking it out to Guns N' Roses
- Loves Lululemon pants
- Loves singlets from Cotton On
- Loves champagne
- Eats sugar-free (most of the time)
- Loves being on her phone
- Hates being so contactable all the time.

Or your hot coal client is a 30-year-old male author who:

- Loves hanging out with the guys
- Loves being alone
- Loves writing
- Dislikes the pressure of writing
- Enjoys being busy
- Enjoys doing nothing
- Is the life of the party
- Doesn't always like to be the centre of attention.

The more you know about your hot coal clients the better off you are, because it's going to make it so easy to create content that resonates with them. You know their problems. You know their goals, dreams and desires. You know that you can help them with what you do.

When you do this, it means you:

- are able to be consistent with your messaging

- help your audience to see that you can empathise with where they're at and what they're going through

- can connect with them in a way that nobody else can

- build trust faster than if you're out there trying to convince people that you know your stuff

- will be seen in their eyes as an expert at what you do.

Now you just need to engage them!

STAGE 2: HOW TO ENGAGE WITH YOUR HOT COAL CLIENTS

Have you ever felt that someone on the internet has had a camera on you, in your home or in your head, listening in to your conversations? *'How are you in my head?'* you ask when you're really engaged with someone online. There is a simple way to make this happen: you just need to actively speak to people in their language to make them hot coal clients.

There is a whole industry built around 'building your engagement' online, which is code for 'pay for more people to like your content'. We're not looking to increase 'visible engagement', where people like, comment and/or share your content. You and I are going to talk about engaging with people in their *heads*. I have literally had clients tell me that they 'stalked' me for years online before commenting or even liking any of my posts – literally years. (I think Cait holds the record. She started following me as far back as 2011, but didn't actually visibly engage with me until 2017!)

When you engage with your hot coal clients in their heads and their hearts, they learn to trust you.

When you do this well, your hot coal clients will feel heard, understood and valued. This is the key to creating rapport: matching what they're thinking in their heads with what they're reading. Rapport is created when you feel like you're 'in sync' with people. You've probably found yourself at different times copying the way a person holds their arms when you've been in deep conversation with them. Or maybe you have noticed the person you're talking to ends up crossing their legs immediately after you do. This indicates that you have a rapport with the other person.

Online, it's a lot harder to know if you're in rapport with someone. The indicators are harder to read, so you do the smart thing: you assume that you're in rapport with them. Additionally, you are going to become an *expert in them.*

CREATING RAPPORT ONLINE WITH DIFFERENT TYPES OF LEARNERS

Human behaviour fascinates me. It always has. The more I read and learn about it, the more fascinated I become. I want to share with you the *keys* to creating rapport and connection online.

There are three main learning styles: visual, auditory and kinaesthetic (see the diagram opposite). Visual people like watching and reading information. Auditory people like to be able to hear you. Kinaesthetic learners like having downloads from you; they like to touch things.

VISUAL

AUDITORY   KINAESTHETIC

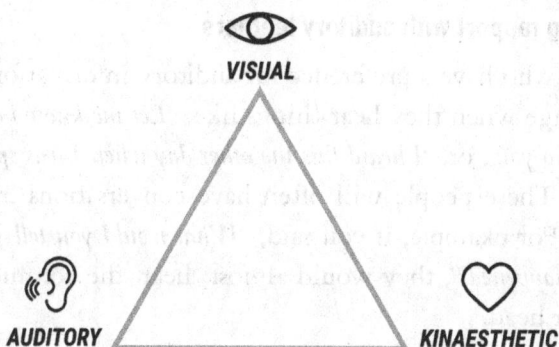

Let's break down how you get inside the heads of all three types of people by speaking and communicating in their language.

Creating rapport with visual learners

Visual people engage a lot with videos, imagery and words. You'll need to use language like, *'You'll see what I mean when I explain this'*, or, *'Did you see what I did there?'*. These kinds of people tend to enjoy picturing things in their head, using sentences like, *'Imagine for a moment a time when you could get inside someone's head'*. They see things in their mind's eye.

Visual people will often close their eyes while they're learning, so they can visualise in their head what you're talking about.

✳ ACTIVITY: Communicating with visual learners

Think about how you would communicate with your hot coal clients if you knew that their primary way of learning was through visual mediums. For instance, you could use posters, infographics, photos, other styles of images, grids, videos and live streams.

Creating rapport with auditory learners

People who have a preference for auditory information tend to engage when they hear things like, *'Let me know how this sounds to you'*, or, *'I heard this the other day when I was speaking to Jill'*. These people will often have conversations in their heads! For example, if you said, *'What would you tell yourself if this happened?'*, they would almost 'hear' the commentary in their head.

Auditory people often feel as if they need to repeat what has been said or explain it back to someone in order for it to get into their brain.

✳ *ACTIVITY: Communicating with auditory learners*

Think about how you would communicate with your hot coal clients if you knew that their primary way of learning was through audible mediums. For instance, you could create a podcast, ensure you use live streams, create a jingle for an acronym that you've created or have them listen to you while you share stories.

Creating rapport with kinaesthetic learners

People who are predisposed to this method of absorbing information tend to be the 'feelers' in your audience. *'How does this make you feel?'* or *'Feels good, doesn't it, to be warm?'* They are very experience-driven. You'd consider creating downloads for them to touch with their hands and encourage them to take notes.

Kinaesthetic people tend to shuffle their hands. They play with a stress ball or a pen while they're thinking. It opens up the gateway to learning for them.

✳ ACTIVITY: Communicating with kinaesthetic learners

Think about how you would communicate with your hot coal clients if you knew that their primary way of learning was through kinaesthetic mediums. For instance, you could encourage them to write things down, to walk while they're listening to your live stream replay or have them role-play a concept that you introduce. The movement helps them to shortcut the processing of the information.

I have found in my workshops and events over the years that my audience is pretty evenly split across the board (30 per cent of each type of learner). However, some people are a mix of two predominant styles. Among my clients, I have approximately 30 per cent of mixed (i.e. auditory and visual) learners.

CREATING RAPPORT ONLINE WITH DIFFERENT BEHAVIOURAL TYPES

To further understand your hot coal clients, we're going to look at the DISC® model of human behaviour. DISC® is an acronym for Dominant, Inspiring, Supportive and Cautious but I have a slight variation on this. My model interprets DISC as: Dominant, Influential, Safety/Security and Compliant (see the model below).

```
                    ↑
   COMPLIANT    │    DOMINANT

←───────────────┼───────────────→

SAFETY/SECURITY │    INFLUENTIAL
                    ↓
```

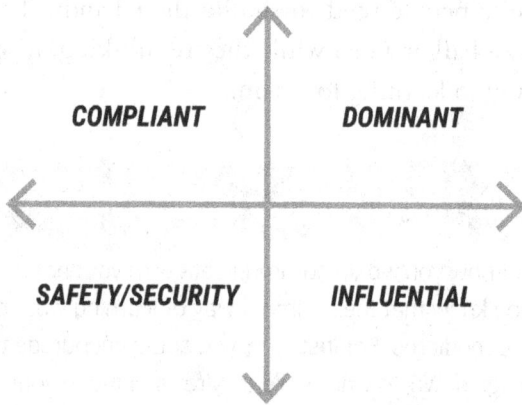

I am going to share with you a big picture view of each of these types. I encourage you to work out which type best describes your type of client. (Remember that 30 per cent of your clients are likely to be a combination of two types.)

Dominant types

People who identify with this particular behavioural type are driven by winning and success. They generally make fast decisions when they see that it's going to help them be better, raise to the top and ultimately win. These kinds of people like to hear how your services are going to help them win and succeed even more. They tend to see something once, and make a decision on it straight away.

When you're marketing yourself and stepping into the spotlight (which we'll get more into in chapter 6 don't worry!), it's crucial that you help this type of person make decisions fast. If things are too long-winded and they don't have the opportunity to make fast decisions, you can lose them.

✳ ACTIVITY: Communicating with dominants

If you are talking to someone personally, you could ask them questions about what drives them. For example, 'Are you more motivated by winning/succeeding or by getting things right?'. The answer will help you to determine if they fit the dominant category.

Influential types

Influential type people love being on stage, performing and being the centre of attention. For them to make decisions, they need to hear how what you have to offer is going to help them get that exposure. They need to know that other people are coming along on 'the party bus' as well!

People who fall into this category like to hear all the stories about what you've got to offer. They want to hear success stories. They also love to talk, so it's important that they feel as if they have a say.

✳ ACTIVITY: Communicating with influencers

If you are talking to someone personally and you suspect that they might fit primarily into this category, you could ask them questions such as, 'Do you love being the centre of attention?', or, 'Have you dreamed of being on stage either online or offline and helping many people?', or, 'When you make decisions about buying, is it important for you to know that there are going to be other people who you can interact and have fun with?'. If they say yes to any of these, then you've got yourself someone who fits in the 'influential' category.

When you're marketing to influencers and stepping into the spotlight it's crucial that you share stories with them about who else is going to be a part of what you're doing – or who has previously been a part of what you're doing. They want to see that they're going to have fun as well as learn things that will help them succeed. They will also want to be recognised as succeeding.

Safety/security types

This type tends to be very concerned about safety and security. They will generally not interact with you at all visibly until they feel they can trust you – and they are very slow to trust. However, once they do trust you, they'll trust you for life (unless you do the wrong thing by them, and that's a different story!). They're very loyal. They also like to know who has gone before them. They don't like being a test case. They like to hear assurances like, 'it's been tried and tested'.

In your marketing to safety types of people, it's important to share photos and testimonials of others you've worked with. They look for the social proof. They can also be known to be 'mis-matchers' – they look for reasons to *not* trust you.

✳ *ACTIVITY: Communicating with safety types*

If you're talking to a safety-driven type personality, you might ask them if they tend to hang back before making decisions. Are they watchers and observers? You could ask them if they are known in their circles as being very loyal and the nurturer of the group.

When you're marketing yourself, it's important that you let these types know they're safe and that you have their back. These people tend to be risk-averse. They tend to look for the reasons to *distrust* you rather than the reasons to trust you. Be consistent, always. Be *you* all of the time and you will win them over! They are very slow to make decisions because they're so driven by safety, so buckle up for the long haul.

Compliant types

People who fall into this category are people who prefer being alone to do the methodical work that they do best. Compliant people love numbers, case studies, data and cold, hard facts. They don't tend to buy into too much story.

They can get overwhelmed by detail and just shut down. To help them, it's important to share case studies and data in your marketing.

✳ **ACTIVITY: Communicating with compliant types**

If you're talking to a person who typically identifies as a compliant type, you can ask them what kinds of data they like to read. Ask if they'd like to read case studies or testimonials. Some of the clues that your client falls in this segment are that they'll often ask for more information in order to make a decision. Ask them if they have done their research or if they need more time to do it.

With the marketing you'll be doing (don't worry, it's coming!) you just have to think of ways to incorporate something for each behavioural type: for instance, a case study or a statistic;

or evidence about other people who this has worked for; or a story about how it came about. Make it really easy for others to make a fast decision.

STAGE 3: HOW TO ACTIVATE YOUR CLIENTS

Now that you know exactly how to connect with and engage your hot coal clients, it's time to activate them.

Think of this phase as if you've got the washing powder ready. You've got the clothes in the washer. But until you put the powder in and turn the machine on, those clothes will not get clean! The washing powder gets activated by the water that's in the machine. And then the clothes come out sparkly and fresh.

You need to activate the people you've identified clearly as those you want to work with. You need to get them *doing* something, taking some type of action with you. It could be that you ask them to comment on a blog or on one of your social media posts. Maybe you can ask them to give you their email address in exchange for a free resource that you've put together.

If you miss this step, they'll get all excited as they feel like you know them because you've connected with them. They'll feel valued because you've engaged them by talking to them in their language, but if you don't *do* something with them now, if you don't lead them to the next step, they'll probably forget you.

When people aren't activated, they get distracted by the next shiny person who comes along and talks their language.

They forget you. And you'll find that you're back, trying to busk to everyone in the hope of being thrown a dollar.

At this point, consider what they need in the world. You know what their problems are. You know what their desires are. You need to be the bridge (your content will be the bridge) that will help close the gap for them. In this phase you need to create free things that you can give away, such as:

- PDFs
- Guides
- eBooks
- Books
- Webinars
- Checklists

- Seminars
- Discovery sessions
- Podcasts
- Videos
- Video training.

Think about it from a famous musician's perspective. They appear in magazines so people can put photos of them up on their walls. They release an album. They have their songs played on the radio. They design t-shirts and other merchandise for fans to purchase. All of this happens *before* they release concert dates. They're on *Video Hits* and *Rage*. You get to hear their music without spending money or for a relatively low investment. This is how they activate their audience, getting them excited for what's to come.

When you get to this stage in setting yourself up for stepping into the spotlight, you have a solid foundation before you even get out there to *enhance* what you're doing out there.

The payoff for doing this hard work is you know your hot coal clients better than they know themselves. This is the start of your positioning. This is the way that you can build and grow your expert status. This is the way that you can be seen as a specialist.

You rock.

INTERVIEW WITH MODERN FOLK SINGER AMY SPEACE

Award-winning modern folk singer Amy Speace appears fearless – whether she's on Broadway or a smaller stage with her guitar. She shared in her interview that, for her, stepping into the spotlight was in her DNA. But she still has moments on stage when her inner critic and the muse battle it out. The negative self-talk can start up, but she no longer allows that to throw her off.

At times she shares with her audience, with brave vulnerability, what is happening – that she's forgotten a lyric or she's having a battle with herself. And her audience loves her for that. You see, she knows them. She knows that there are people in the audience who need to hear her music on that particular day, and it's for them that she shows up.

Amy shared her number one piece of advice for people like you who are stepping out: work with a mentor and practise your craft every single day.

To read/hear the full interview, make sure you head to www.nicolamoras.com.au/intothespotlight

CHAPTER SUMMARY

YOU NEED TO FIND YOUR AUDIENCE.

LEARN HOW TO BUILD YOUR RELATIONSHIPS FROM *'I DON'T KNOW YOU'* TO *'I WANT TO BUY FROM YOU'.*

VISUALISE YOUR HOT COAL CLIENTS.

ENGAGE WITH THE DIFFERENT TYPES OF LEARNERS AND TYPES OF CLIENT BEHAVIOURS.

DON'T MISS THE VITAL STEP OF ACTIVATING YOUR HOT COAL CLIENTS.

SIX
BE THE
ROCK STAR

YOU FIND YOURSELF in the backstage area of a stadium. You have a lanyard around your neck that has given you access. You look around and see your friends. You see the production team. There's crew everywhere in their black t-shirts and jeans (the mandatory 'roadie uniform'). There's a low energetic hum of excitement and anticipation. You know something amazing is happening and you're standing right in the middle of it.

You close your eyes for a moment and tilt your head back slightly as you take in the smell of popcorn from the concession stands. You can almost taste the popcorn in your mouth and the salt on your lips. You can hear people talking excitedly. You can feel the energy pulsing through the room. Your heart is beating fast. It's as if all your senses are heightened – you feel so alert.

You open your eyes and start walking towards the corridor where there are doors on either side, stretching as far as you can see. You walk calmly down the corridor noting the names on the doors and then you stop. You turn to face one of the doors. There's a big star on the door... and it has your name on it.

Your heart beats faster still as you turn the knob and step inside. The room is luxurious. It's huge and there are people milling around, fussing with makeup, getting outfits ready. There are wigs, hair dryers and straighteners all over the bench where you're about to get ready. You take the seat you're directed to and you look at yourself in the Hollywood mirror on the wall. It's so surreal! You have been dreaming of being able to do this for most of your life and 'suddenly' it's happening. You're here. This *is really* happening.

The makeup artists and hair stylists get to work. You watch the transformation unfold in front of your eyes. It's so exciting. Your family come in and sit on the couches that are set up in the room and they too watch excitedly as you prepare and get ready. The music is on, it's playing your favourite tunes and the butterflies of excitement start. Admittedly, you're a little nervous, but you know that this just means you care about what's about to happen – you care deeply. What's about to transpire is something you'll never forget.

When the hair and makeup team is finished with you, you make your way to the clothing rack where the costumes await. There are sequins upon sequins, body suits, jeans, heels, booty shorts, corsets, jackets, gowns – the works. One of the team takes a look at the running sheet and hands you the first costume that you're going to wear. You put it on, knowing that you're in the best shape of your whole damn life. You look freaking amazing. You feel amazing. You have more energy today than you had in your twenties. You are gorgeous and, damn it, you know it.

As you're about to leave the dressing room, you take a look in the mirror and you are in awe at the reflection that stares back at you. You're miked up and ready to go. The butterflies that were there before have turned into 'let's just get this started!'. It reminds you a bit of your wedding day, when you wanted to run down the aisle to meet your soon-to-be-husband but had to hold back because 'it was the done thing' to walk s-l-o-w-l-y down the aisle!

You make your way to the bottom of a staircase. As you look up the stairs, you feel a rush of air. You can hear people talking, clapping, singing and stomping their feet. That's all for you. The audience can't wait. The air is thick with anticipation. You wait for the 'nod' from the stage manager and you hear the MC over the speakers ask the audience to stand and to make the most noise they can to welcome you onto the stage. All you hear is a loud ROOOOOOAAARRRRRRRR unlike anything you've ever heard before. You walk up the stairs and onto the stage, where you're about to do the very thing that you were put on this earth to do: to help every single person in the audience with what you do.

Let the show begin.

Stepping into the spotlight

WTF! You want me to do what?

Being online and stepping into your spotlight takes courage. It takes bravery. What you're going to learn in this part of the book is *why* it's more important than ever to overcome your worries and your fears about being seen and *be visible*.

I'm going to teach you how to do it! Yay! You'll eliminate any and all excuses. You are going to be like Nike and *Just Do It*, because you'll have a plan and you'll know how to implement it.

But first, the bravery barometer.

Bravery barometer

Take a look at the graphic. I need to move you from being in fear of being in the spotlight to feeling unstoppable, as you were at the bottom of the steps before you walked onto the stage. Everything that we go through is designed to move you closer to feeling unstoppable.

Most people are afraid to put themselves out there because they're worried about what their peers might say or how they might come across. They are afraid of not having the words when the camera is rolling or feeling as if they look like an idiot online. They fear that they might say something wrong and offend someone; or even that they'll not be able to inspire people to work with them and it will end up being a big fat waste of time, money and energy.

It's okay. It's not just you who has these little pesky thoughts and worries. Welcome to being human! To step into the spotlight you have to step out of your comfort first. The spotlight can be hot, bright and shiny – and the great thing is that, when you're in it, your audience will see you shine.

But I like being invisible.

No, you don't. Not really. Not when you know that being online is the way that you're going to help your audience. It's the way that they're going to find you. It's the way you're going to connect with them and it's the way that you're going to build solid, sustainable relationships with them online.

People are less trusting than they once were, and their bullshit detectors are on super-high-alert. They can smell someone who is being inauthentic a mile away. People are trusting CEOs and government agencies less and less, and it's more important than ever for people to find others (like you) who they can learn to trust online. They want you to have their back. They are looking for people who are willing to step up and lead the way from a place of vulnerability and humility.

The other benefit to being in the spotlight is that you'll create influence. I'm not talking about becoming an 'influencer' – someone who gets paid to travel and eat at certain restaurants, or to wear particular jewellery or active wear! I'm suggesting that when you step into the spotlight and utilise the three major strategies that we'll talk about later in the book, you'll create influence. When you create influence, people listen when you speak. When you ask them to do something, they'll do it.

Consider the Live Aid concert. Queen graced the stage at Live Aid and, by doing so, inspired many thousands of people to pick up their phones and donate for the relief of famine in African nations. That concert raised $127 million. That's influence.

It's crucial at this point for you to create your own intellectual property, which we're going to explore at length throughout this chapter. It's important that you make the commitment to being even more brave (if that's possible!) than you were a minute ago. Rock stars get out there and say what they want to say with strength and confidence – and to hell with anyone who happens to disagree with them! They're not bothered about everyone liking them. They are there to share their message, their voice and their tunes with the world and with those who choose to listen to them. When you share your opinions, your thoughts – and why you came up with these thoughts – are important things for the world to hear. It really is all about you at this stage.

BUT, HOW DO I *BECOME* THE ROCK STAR?

Don't just try to emulate a rock star, *become* a rock star.

There are three main activities you need to do to really bring the rock star vibe online (and offline, for that matter):

1. You need to bring the **energy**

2. You need to work on your **positioning**

3. You need to work on the **platforms** that you show up on (which we cover in chapter 7).

We're going to work through each of these systematically, because they are all co-dependent. Each is as important as the other, and just as a three-legged table would fall over if one leg were missing, you need all three pillars under you to support your efforts as you step into the spotlight.

You know how you see some people and you just gasp because they have that 'star quality'. There's an air and a look about them and they've got the 'tude. (It's not a bad attitude – it could be that they're confident or aloof or just downright nice and they don't have any airs or graces about them at all.) Yet, they have that otherworldly, starlike quality.

You know exactly who I mean. They might not even be a celebrity. There are some people who I've come across in my own social media feeds and I hesitate for a second in my scrolling because there's just something about their post. It could be the imagery they've used, the words they've shared or the way they created a rock star first impression. I'm sure you've seen it too. Think red carpet screen sirens. Think the mothers you know who always seem to have it together and exude confidence and charm.

Do you want the good news? You can create this. You can cultivate it. You can practise it. You can *become* it.

Let's do it.

IT ALL STARTS WITH ENERGY

Remember at the start of the chapter, we were talking about you being in the stadium, preparing to walk up the steps to the stage to give the performance of your life? I want you to take yourself back to that moment. Imagine that you can feel the certainty in your bones. You're grounded and confident. You know the whole stadium of people is waiting there for *you.* You've been preparing for this moment for your whole life. You can feel the collective energy.

This is where you develop your rock star stance.

Many coaches, trainers and consultants will suggest that you research your competitors to see what they're doing. They'll recommend that you check out their pricing.

Do I suggest you do that? Oh, hell no! Comparison is evil! When you start looking at what other people are doing, it's too easy to get swayed into trying to be better than them, do better than them. I want you to differentiate yourself from them.

Comparison is the breeding ground for imposter syndrome and you have no time for that.

There is more than enough business to go around. I can guarantee you that, just because someone else in your industry 'seems' to be successful, it doesn't mean that they are. They're out there showing the world what they want to show the world, not necessarily what the reality is.

Nobody wants to feel substandard compared to anyone else in their industry. Nobody wants to feel as if they have to look to others and compare where they're at. If you don't develop your own feeling of rock star energy first, you run the risk of coming across as wobbly, uncertain and unconfident. Your audience might think you lack substance and certainty, which diminishes the trust they have in you and what you have to say. It erodes the foundations of what you've been building, so make sure you work on this.

Use this mantra to remember your rock star quality. You are:

Radiant

Opinionated

Charismatic

Kickass

Sexy

Talented

Attitude

Rock star!

And while we're at it, here are some suggestions to bring in the rock star energy:

► Love yourself first

► Channel your favourite rock star

► Create your rock star stance

► Use that stance.

How do you want to come across while you're delivering your message?

You need to get comfortable being uncomfortable; feel the fear and do it anyway – and all the other clichés that you know tie into all of this. (The magic begins at the edge of your comfort zone, for example! Sorry, I couldn't resist another one!)

At first, you might feel a little weird when you decide that you're going to channel Gwen Stefani or Freddie Mercury, Lady Gaga or Robbie Williams. But here's the thing, my friend: people love the heck out of entertainers. They love the drama they build, the presence they bring to the stage, the way they don't hold back.

Create an alter ego

Many performers create an alter ego. Beyoncé has talked extensively about the use of her alter ego, Sasha Fierce, who was her performance personality who allowed her the creative licence to experiment on stage with different things. Sasha served her for years until she told MTV in an interview in 2010 that *'Sasha Fierce is done. I killed her'.*

When you're thinking about everything you're being called to do, which might feel wildly uncomfortable and unfamiliar, step into an alter ego who loves the spotlight. Give them a name, give them a personality. When you feel like you've grown into that person, as if you've merged these two personalities together, retire the alter ego!

Remember that it takes time, consistency and practice to be able to bring this in, but YOU ARE A ROCK STAR and it's now time to start to show up like one.

A way to really step into your rock star energy is to come up with a word (or words) that you can embody, to almost create a persona that you step into when you're creating everything that you'll use to step into the spotlight. The activity below will help you with this.

✳ ACTIVITY: Find your words

You're going to come up with a list of words that you love, words that inspire you and motivate you, words that push you to step into the most ambitious, amazing version of *you*.

Some examples of words/phrases that clients of mine have come up with are:

- Bullshit slayer
- Powerfully unleashed
- Forged (like steel)
- Unstoppable
- Phoenix rising
- Infinite

- Impact
- Power personified
- Calm
- Grounded
- Hell yes!
- Adventure.

When you have chosen your word(s), find an A4 piece of paper and write your word in the middle of the page, as large as you can. This is going to be your word that gets you through at least the next 12 months. It's the word that you'll use to remind yourself of your amazingness. You'll use it to remind yourself to step into the spotlight, even when you're afraid – or if you're nervous or not feeling it.

This is the word that says: *'This is who I am. I am [WORD]'.*

Say it out loud. Say, *'This is who I am. I am [WORD]'.* Say it again. Plant your feet firmly on the ground, take a big breath in and say it again: *'This is who I am. I am [WORD]. THIS is who I am. I AM [WORD].'*

How freaking powerful does that feel?

The reason that you're doing this is because it gives you a feeling of power, strength and being grounded, which will serve you when self-doubt hits.

This word will remind you at any given time who you are from a place of power.

Feelings and actions are powerful anchors, just like smells. An anchor is described as *'a trigger or stimulus that retrieves a desired emotional state'* and it is super-powerful. When you think about the smell of freshly mowed grass, you get a mental image that takes you back to a time when you remember the same smell. You can see in your mind what the day was like when you smelled that smell. Who was near you? What time of day was it? Who had mowed the lawn? You can take a trip down memory lane and smell that smell in your imagination, and see it in your imagination. It's like travelling back in time.

What you're invoking when you anchor *your word* is the feeling of being unstoppable. It gives you the chance to get it in your body and access it at any time.

The next thing to do is choose a song that enforces this word and this feeling. Some of my favourites are 'Don't stop believin'' by Journey, 'The show must go on' by Queen and 'What you waiting for?' by Gwen Stefani.

What are yours?

LET'S WORK ON YOUR POSITIONING

Now you are developing your rock star energy, we need to work on the second activity: your positioning.

More and more artists are making it into the music charts all the time, playing new songs. New and upcoming artists are being honoured at industry awards, and the veterans keep releasing new albums too. Yet, we don't complain that someone else just released a song, so we can't possibly release one as well.

So often, I've heard: *'There are so many people already in my industry doing xyz, how on earth am I going to stand out and why do I need to bother?'*. If you've uttered those words, you're certainly not alone. And, let's be honest with each other: the online world is even more noisy than it was six months ago, and in six months from now it will be even louder.

Positioning is the key to standing out.

How do you build your positioning? It's not rocket science, but it does take some time to map out. Positioning is made of up three things:

1. Your message
2. Your intellectual property
3. Getting this out there.

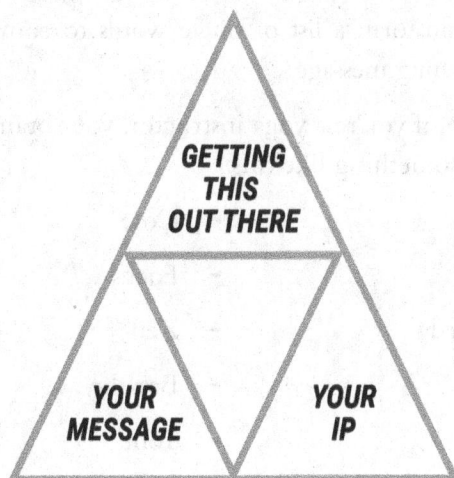

```
                    /\
                   /  \
                  /    \
                 / GETTING \
                /  THIS  \
               / OUT THERE \
              /_____\
             /\            /\
            /  \          /  \
           /    \        /    \
          / YOUR \      / YOUR \
         / MESSAGE\    /  IP   \
        /_____\  /_____\
```

Your message

Your message is the ribbon that links and ripples through everything you do in your marketing, when you're building your online presence and the way you show up in the world.

Remember your word that you anchored just before with your rock star energy? Keep that close to you, as that is key to your message. Now you need to decide what your overall message is.

Here's where you get to play!

I want you to consider these questions:

- What is the overarching 'thing' that you do for your audience?

- What is the main outcome that you create for your audience?

You can brainstorm a list of single words to come up with your overarching message.

For example, if you're a yoga instructor, your brainstorm list could look something like this:

- Calm
- Centred
- Grounded
- Mindful
- Stretch
- Strong

- Core
- Focus
- Zen
- Breathe
- Tone
- Mindfulness.

Or, if you're a graphic designer and you help people with their visual branding, your list might be like this:

- Powerful
- Brave
- Magnetic
- Inspiring
- Motivated
- Polished
- Professional
- Clickable
- Strong
- Stand-out.

It takes time to brainstorm these words. Here's how you can do it.

Imagine that you're in the airport on the way to a conference that you've been hanging out to get to for the past six months. You have whisked your way through security (thank goodness for the Frequent Flyer line!) and you're heading to the lounge to relax, have a coffee and catch up with your emails before boarding your flight. Before hitting the lounge, you meander through some clothes stores and find yourself at the airport bookstore. You're staring at the shelf at the end of the stand where a big sign says 'Bestselling books this month' – and there is *your* book in the Top Ten (probably sitting at number one, because you are a bad-ass!). You look at it in disbelief. You worked on this book for so long. You went through the processes of writing, editing, more editing, choosing covers, to getting the proof copy in your hands, and now it's in the bookstore as you'd always dreamed.

I want you to see that book. Look at it. What is the single word (at the most, a maximum of two words) title of that book? Now, pick up the book. Feel it in your hands. Turn it over so you can see the spine, the back cover and, of course, you have to flick the pages to smell that new-book smell. You did it! You're so clever.

What is the name of the book?

Usually when I step people through this process, they instinctively think of a singular word (perhaps two) and this is a pretty good indicator of what their overarching message will be.

Take some time to brainstorm what your word is, keeping your hot coal clients in mind. What is it that you do for them? What specifically do you help them with?

Now that you have your word, everything that you create is going to tie in with that word. All the content that you put out there online (which we'll talk about soon, don't worry!) is going to lead back to this word.

You are doing this because it helps you to focus and create consistency.

CASE STUDY: Gerda Muller

Gerda needed a marketing 'angle' for a conference she wanted to put on for allied health professionals in Australia. She wanted something that was going to be unique and powerful and really stand out from anything anyone had ever seen before. She wanted to make a big splash and create a point of difference from all the other professional development conferences out there. She brainstormed some words and came up with a central theme: *Elevate*.

Elevate became the name of her conference. All her content, stories, promotions – yes, everything – revolved around Elevate:

BE THE ROCK STAR

elevate your mindset, your business, your knowledge and your support team.

Having this one, single word made her messaging and her marketing consistent. It made it easy for her to step into the spotlight with the marketing that she did for this conference.

Your power statement

Now you are going to create a simple statement that you can use anywhere and everywhere – especially on your website! Here's an activity to help you create your power statement.

✳ ACTIVITY: Creating your power statement

I help .... *[insert WHO you help]*

.... *[do what?]*

by .... *[how do you help them?]*

so they can .... *[do what?]*.

My mission is to .... *[why do I do this?]*.

I do this by .... *[how do I do this?]*.

For example, if you are a motivational speaker who works with executives to improve their productivity and sales, your power statement might be:

I help successful executives increase their productivity and sales by growing their confidence and skills.

My mission is to help improve the quality of people's lives. I do this by 1:1 consulting, coaching and bespoke training programs for individuals and businesses.

INTERVIEW WITH JESSI ALEXANDER, COUNTRY MUSIC SINGER

Jessi was sitting on her porch in Nashville and I was sitting at my desk in Mildura, just two country folks jamming about everything to do with stepping into the spotlight. In my mind's eye, I imagined that I was there with her, sitting on her porch with a cup of tea, asking her about her journey into the spotlight and how she came to be where she is today.

I have to admit, when I was researching Jessi (to make sure I didn't make a total fool of myself in this interview) I really enjoyed seeing photos of her and her family on social media, playing together and looking like they were having the time of their lives. The photos she shared of her children and her husband were a sneak peek behind the scenes of her life as a country music singer and songwriter. I got the feeling that this was what inspired her on a daily basis. The glimpse I got of her personal world made me feel as if I already knew her, and this made the conversation that ensued flow in the most lovely way.

Jessi made a big leap this year, during the COVID-19 pandemic, when she released her latest album 'Decatur County Red', without a record label, without a tour and without doing any of the 'normal' things an artist does to promote their work. This meant she had to rely on publicity and social media to sell records – and it's proven to be something of a learning curve. Jessi admits to preferring to be in the background rather than in the spotlight. She knew that she needed to take a more 'front and centre' role with her social media but she needed to be authentic and treat her social media as an extension of who she is.

Jessi fell in love with music as a child and it became a means of escape. She worked hard. She made so many sacrifices that many kids (or adults) wouldn't have made to get to where she is. Her achievements include number one records, Hall of Fame notoriety, opening shows with Sheryl Crow and writing songs for a slew of artists (including Miley Cyrus, Blake Shelton, Lee Brice and Travis Denning) – some that were hits and others that were not.

Many might say she's 'made it'. But Jessi shared that for her, success is less about being competitive with everyone else and more about striving for and achieving what she wants for herself. For her, success is about going all in, fighting the 'good fight' and sometimes you'll win the knockout! Most importantly, it's about creating songs that affect people and that mean something.

When I asked for her advice on stepping into the spotlight and chasing down success, she said this:

- 'The thing that successful people have in common is persistence and perseverance. You've got to be ambitious, too, otherwise someone is going to take your spot!'

- 'Hunger and passion are necessary if you want to succeed. You're going to get discouraged and frustrated. You need these two things to fall back on. If you think of this as some kind of job, then it's going to be a harder road when you have disappointments.'

- 'You've got to work hard and play hard. But you've also got to be fully engaged with what you're doing when you're doing it.'

- 'Many people will tell you not to, and I've used all of those naysayers to light and fuel my fire. For every person that said I should have moved home or that I couldn't do it or that I was done... I look at them as a gift. It's not to say that these things don't sting and hurt, but you have to dust yourself off, move on and forge ahead.'

- 'There are a lot of reasons to quit. You'll get bored. You'll get discouraged and you'll get frustrated. You cannot let these defeat your passion and hunger.'

- 'Preparation and purpose are KEY to you getting to where you want to be. In fact, when opportunity and preparation meet, it's like magic. I work tirelessly daily on my craft so, when an opportunity comes, I am ready and confident.'

- 'Don't chase someone else's art. This can be a huge thing that can make you self-conscious. Purpose was literally put into your heart, the talent and gifts were placed in your hands. Honour that.'

I know that the image a lot of people portray is one of confidence and an 'I've got this' kind of attitude. For Jessi, performing her music has always been something she's comfortable with. However, she did say that when she has to give a speech (like at a number one party) the nerves kick in. What gets her through is reminding herself that this is what she was born to do. To prepare, she'll pray, get grounded and listen to some music that transports her to a place where she can get through it.

Jessi sees music as a way to make a difference in someone's life or to move them. Even if it's just one person in the crowd, then 'it's worth it to me,' she admits. 'It's not about being the winner or being number one, I just want to be looked at as a great songwriter'.

This is what you are striving for in your visibility efforts. If you can impact even one person in a positive way, with what you put out there today (and every day!), then it has to be worth it.

Remember always to share things online that aren't necessarily just about 'buy my stuff'. Share behind-the-scenes you, because that helps your audience feel like they are getting to know who you are as a person, as an artist, as a business owner.

When preparation and opportunity meet, that's when the magic happens.

CHAPTER SUMMARY

CREATE YOUR POWER WORD.

WORK OUT YOUR OVERARCHING WORD/THEME.

CREATE YOUR POWER STATEMENT.

SEVEN
WHERE
ROCK STARS
HANG OUT

THE THIRD PART in the process of becoming a rock star is deciding where to show up. You don't want to be the opera singer playing to a stadium of heavy rock fans (remember?). This is the part of becoming visible that most people struggle with. It is so easy to say, *'I'm running a business, I don't have time for all this'*. But really, *if you don't have time for all this, you won't be running a business (for much longer)*.

Before we go through where you need to be visible, you have to have content to post. Let's take a look at this first.

YOUR INTELLECTUAL PROPERTY

Now that you have your overarching message clear and you know what your power word is (say it again for me: *'This is who I am. I am [word]'*), it's time to work on the creation of your own intellectual property.

> **Intellectual property (IP) is intangible property that is the result of creativity.**

Your intellectual property is your ideas, your research and even the way that you articulate your opinions, which you present in different formats – for instance, your posts, your courses, your marketing, your writing and your videos.

What you're going to do in this chapter is get really clear on how you're going to articulate and create what it is that you ultimately do for people. You're going to come up with your own way of helping your audience get the outcomes they desire. This will create the foundation for all the content that you create from here on out, from your marketing to courses to events to your next book!

There are six parts to your IP.

IP Part 1

First things first, you need to think about the four main stages that you help your people with. For instance, you might take people from feeling really stuck and unclear to feeling really empowered and powerful. If you're a personal trainer, you might help people go from feeling unfit and lethargic to feeling strong and energised.

CASE STUDY: A life coach

A lot of people out there need a life coach to help make decisions for their future. Thelma is a life coach who specialises in helping people who want something more out of their lives, but they're not sure what that is. They're confused and overwhelmed by the choices out there. Do they apply for a promotion? Do they go back to university and study some more? Do they just quit and take a year off to 'find themselves'?

It can be helpful for people to talk this kind of thing through, because there are many perceived barriers to making decisions about changing your life. There are financial considerations, family obligations, location constraints and just plain confusion because, of course, everyone has an opinion on what you should do with your life.

Thelma helps people by taking them from feeling overwhelmed and confused to being confident enough to make decisions. She teaches them to manage their mindset and their self talk, and shows them where to find the resources they need.

A key word for Thelma was 'Adventure', so everything that she does revolves around that.

The four stages Thelma helps her clients through are:

1. The call to adventure (should I change career or not?!)

2. How do I get there? (You need a map)

3. Go there! (Plug in the GPS and create an action plan)

4. Speed bumps a-plenty! (Navigating obstacles when they come up).

Now it's your turn: start with the big-picture four stages that you know you have to work through with your audience. Understand that each of these stages can be broken down further, which we'll do next.

NOTE: There are worksheets that I have created to help you create your web of awesomeness. You can download these from www.nicolamoras.com.au/intothespotlight. There's a video that I created to go along with it. It looks like the image below.

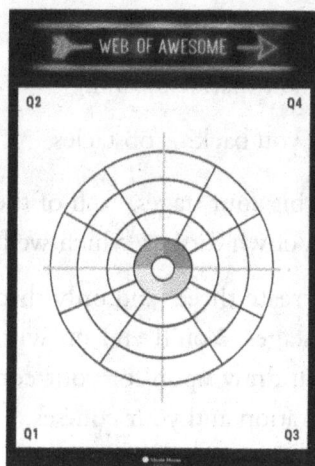

Please note that creating the first part of your IP can take some time. It's not always a quick activity. Give yourself permission to play with it. The best advice I can give you, though, is to start. You can always rework it later.

IP Part 2

Now that you have your four stages mapped out, the next thing to do is to break this down. Like any good song, there are many layers to it. You hear the lyrics and the music as a whole. But you can also narrow down the sounds to recognise individual instruments, riffs and melodies. It's amazing how many components there are to just one piece of music.

Like music, your intellectual property runs deep and you are going to drill down to the next layer. Starting with your first stage, I want you to work out the three components that you would do with your clients to help them get to that first stage.

Using Thelma's case study for example, the first stage (the call to adventure) could be broken down into:

1. What do you want? – motivators

2. Why do you want that? – meaning

3. What has held you back? – obstacles.

Then, as with the big four stages, each of these three categories can be broken down further, which we'll get into shortly.

Go through and create three (and only three) categories for each of the four stages. You'll end up with twelve defined topics that you can draw upon for your content, your marketing, your inspiration and your courses.

IP Part 3

I'm sure you've probably worked out what you need to do now! You are a smart cookie, after all. Yes, you're going to break each of these down further. This part is where you articulate what you're actually going to do with hot coal clients in each of these stages. You're going to come up with four activities or topics to work through.

Using Thelma's example of *What do you want?* motivators, the next set of questions might look like:

- What is that you really want – vision activity

- What are the triggers to wanting to change/this call to adventure – triggers

- What are you passionate about? And why?

- Do you understand your drivers – your core values and motivations?

This section is limited only by your expertise, your imagination and your creativity.

IP Part 4

Now that you're really fleshing out your IP, you'll start to see that the way you do things is vastly different to the way anyone else does things. You have opinions on what people need to do in each stage. You have expertise in different areas. There are likely to be activities or techniques that you have learned or you've participated in, that you can use in these sections.

Part 4 is all about the threats to your hot coal clients if they don't do the things that you have outlined in parts 2 and 3.

For example, if you choose not to do the work on your positioning, the threats are that you could end up blending in with the rest of the crowd online and you'll remain invisible. You run the risk of sounding untrained and lacking confidence. The other threats are rejection and even burnout, because instead of creating your positioning online as a specialist, you try to be all things to all people.

IP Part 5

You are getting so deep, and I am so incredibly proud of you. This 'stuff' is exactly what most business owners shy away from because they're happy to take the wins where they can get them rather being strategic about their marketing and positioning. Brace yourself, because this next part is where you get to have a bit of fun!

I'm usually a 'glass half full' kind of gal, so I want you to roll with me for this next one. Agreed? Ace! Let's do it. Write as many responses to the following questions as you can.

- What pisses you off about your industry?
- What pisses you off about the people who don't buy from you?
- What infuriates you about the things that you feel like you can't change in your industry?
- What do you stand for?
- What do you stand against?
- What do you think needs to change?
- What do you think should stay the same?
- Can you find stories, case studies and data to back it up?

IP Part 6

Now let's get visual. Think of some icons that you can use to demonstrate a 'big picture overview' of your process. Here's my example in the graphic below. I have used a thought bubble to represent being a dreamer about your future in quadrant 1. In quadrant 2, there's an icon of a top hat with money sticking out to represent busking. In quadrant 3, I've got a microphone showing you becoming a rock star and, in quadrant 4, there's an explosion of influence as you become iconic.

The four stages to go from dreamer to online rock star

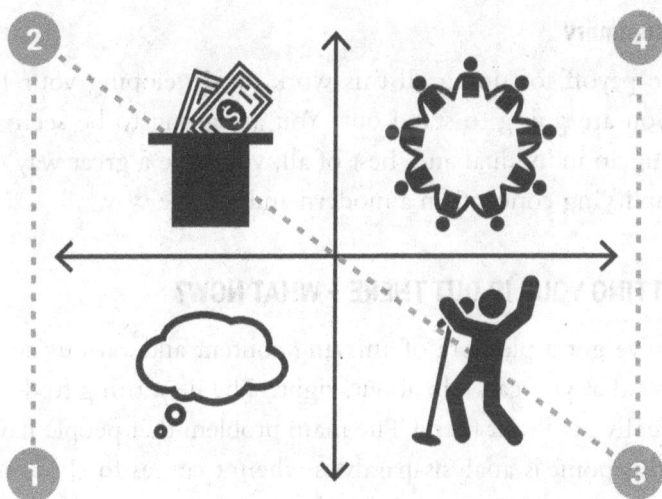

When you have a quick way of explaining your thinking, along with imagery to represent it, it helps the dominant people to make a fast decision about your idea (remember our personality types in chapter 5). It helps the influencers see some of the story and the drama in what you're doing, which they love. The security/safety people see that you have a process, which makes them happy. The compliance people can see a model that you're working through, which helps them to believe in what you're talking about.

Finally, the pictorial representation helps the visual learners; the explanation you give helps the auditory folks and if you make it so people can feel like they get an experience of it by printing it off or downloading it, it helps the kinaesthetic learners as well.

> **Score! You are marketing to all behavioural types and all learning types. #winning**

IP summary

The payoff for doing all this work on developing your IP is you are going to stand out. You are going to be seen as being an individual and, best of all, you have a great way of simplifying concepts in a modern and unique way.

GETTING YOUR IP OUT THERE – WHAT NOW?

You've got a plethora of amazing content and various concepts that you can talk about, right? The next thing to do is actually get it out there! The main problem that people have at this point is analysis-paralysis when it comes to choosing how to use this information online.

The aim of everything you've been doing so far is to get into the spotlight and to stand out. To do that, now you have to get your stuff out there. There is still a lot to consider and many choices to make, though, when it comes to getting out into the online world.

Do you run with Facebook or Instagram? Do you have to learn how to use TikTok or Twitter, or sign up for LinkedIn or Snapchat? The mere thought of having to be present on all of these leaves me rocking in the corner, so I am sure it's overwhelming for you, too.

Contrary to a lot of opinions, you do not have to be on every platform. Many of you don't have a creative team, a social media team, a content production team, a marketing team or a design team. The reality is that there's only you, and there's only so much you can do.

My mission for you, and all business owners, is to help you step into the spotlight *without* having to have all the above teams. I want you to feel confident that you can do it in the least amount of time humanly possible, but in a way that's simple, easy to implement and produces results.

YOUR WEBSITE

You need to have a website that allows you to blog. Blogging is a form of written content (or video content) that helps inspire, motivate or solve a problem for your audience – before they have paid you a cent. *Yes, before they've paid you a cent.* Remember earlier, in chapter 5, we talked about relationship-building online? You need to move your audience from not knowing you at all, to seeing you as someone they trust so they buy from you. You need to become their trusted adviser.

By providing solutions to your online audience in advance (which means you're helping them to move one step closer to the outcome they want) they will get a taste for how you do things, and this will endear them to you. It also helps them to solve a problem, which is a great thing for them, right?

On your website, you will post at least one blog per week. I know! I know! It might feel like a lot but, hey, you've already done the work – because it's what you're going to talk about! Just look back at your IP Part 3, where you listed four topics that you can talk about under each category. This is going to be the topic that you can blog about each week. It will ensure you stay on message and on brand for the whole year! Yes, you've actually mapped out 52 topics to talk about by doing the previous activity! #booyah!

Websites FAQs

I get so many questions about websites. It's easiest for me to share some common FAQs and answer them for you below.

1. Should I blog or vlog and what's the difference?

Blogging is the written form of what you want to share and vlogging (video blogging) is the video format. I always recommend that people do a mix of both. However, if you're just starting out, choose whichever feels the easiest for you. If you can talk under water with a mouth full of marbles, then give vlogging a go! If you feel it's easier for you to write, then get your typing fingers out and give it a whirl. Remember that different people consume information differently (they are visual, auditory and kinaesthetic learners) so it's important to mix it up. Start with whatever is easiest for you.

2. How long should the content be?

Your blog should be as long as it needs to be to get your message across. If you feel it's appropriate to share a short blog of around 350 words — and it gets the message across — then make it 350 words! If it takes 2000 words, then roll with that! There is no right or wrong length. It's as long as it needs to be.

The same answer applies for video blogging (vlogging). It goes for as long as it needs to!

3. How often should I be blogging/vlogging?

If I had my way, I'd have you blogging a few times a week or more, but the key here is consistency. Google's algorithms like it when your website gets updated with new content, so the more often you do that, the more likely you are to improve your rankings. As a general rule of thumb, when you're starting out, make sure you post a blog or vlog at least weekly.

When you're getting the hang of it, do it more regularly — daily would be amazing!

4. Is there a structure to follow?

I love a good framework, so I recommend following this while you build your blogging or vlogging muscle:

- Start with a statement (e.g. Blogging is dead)
- Then share a story about that (e.g. I used to believe it, too, until I tried it!)

  The framework for the story is:

  - Where I was/Where someone else was
  - What I did/What they did
  - Where I am now/Where they are now.

- Talk about the problem that you've seen (e.g. I've seen so many people avoid blogging because they just don't know what to say, how to say it or when to say it. It's super-common and the good news is that we can fix it pretty quickly).

- ► Share the solution with them. Tell them *what* they need to do (e.g. There are four steps to solving this. All you need to is: Step 1: outline your blog; Step 2: work out what story to share; Step 3: work out the problem and the solution for your audience; and Step 4: put it out there).

- ► Have a call to action ready. This could be a program you're running, a course you're doing, an event you're promoting or even a free download that will help them.

5. Do I need fancy equipment like lighting if I want to vlog?

You don't need lighting, but it's great to have it. If you have a smart phone and some good lights that light up that gorgeous face of yours, that's really all the technical studio set up you need.

6. Do I have to employ a web designer/manager to put my blogs up online?

Nope! I would recommend hiring someone to *build* a website for you, though. When I was on maternity leave, I taught myself how to build websites. As my baby was so good, I had copious amounts of time when I was running my first online jewellery business. But, gosh, it took *forever* to do it! My advice now is, *don't do it!* Your time is much better spent doing what you do best: your genius work with your hot coal clients.

FACEBOOK

There are many social media platforms out there, as we've discussed, and I don't want you spending any more time than you need to on social media. After all, it's like the black hole for wasting time for many of us. (Don't look at me!!! Okay, I'm not immune, either!)

I'm starting with Facebook because it is the most *leverageable*.

At the time of writing, Facebook has 2.45 billion monthly active users (and this number is growing). Half of those people are active *daily* on the platform. Your audience is on Facebook. You need to be on Facebook. This is not open for discussion! From therapists to mechanics to authors to accountants to graphic designers to coaches to publishers to yoga instructors to bread makers to IT professionals – you all have to be on Facebook!

Create a business page, if you don't already have one. Ideally this will be in your *name* rather than your company's name. Why? Because people identify more easily with a face. If you hide behind your company name (which I am assuming is different to the name you go by), it can take longer for people to trust you. It also doesn't build your personal brand, which is the whole point of this book: getting YOU into the spotlight.

Facebook FAQs

1. Do I need a business page or can I just use my personal profile?

It's against Facebook's terms of service to use your personal profile for business, so I would avoid that at all costs.

Additionally, you're limited to a maximum of 5000 'friends' on your personal profile. If you want to create a massive impact throughout the world, you don't want to limit yourself to only 5000 connections.

2. What photo should I have as my profile photo?

I get asked this all the time because most people want to be seen as 'real' and at the same time 'professional'. Think about your hot coal clients and what they might like to see. Additionally, go back to your power word and think of an image that invokes those words with your audience.

3. Do I need to have professional photos taken?

No, you don't, but you can if you want to. I had some casual photos taken in 2010 by our family photographer and some others taken by a dear friend's husband that I used for a while. In terms of 'proper' photos, though, I didn't have a professional photo shoot in a 'proper' studio with an actual business brand photographer until 2015. That was five years into my business, when I'd already made millions of dollars online.

A professional photoshoot isn't going to make you more successful, faster. If you feel that it's something you *want* to do and that you can afford, then by all means do it. But, not before you've done the work outlined in this book! When you have your power words, your positioning and your messaging clear, it will help your photographer plan out the shoot with you, and your photos will feel more 'you'. It will help you guide your photographer with how you want your audience to see you, rather than being at the mercy of the photographer taking images of how *they* see you.

4. What category should I choose for my page?

Facebook allows you to pick a category. Choose one that best suits you, from Entrepreneur to Artist to Author to Local Business. You can always change it down the track, so don't sweat the small stuff.

5. How do I get followers/fans/likes?

This is a biggie! The best thing you can focus on is putting up your content (which we'll talk about shortly). From there, you'll start to get fans. It doesn't *really* matter how many 'fans' or 'followers' you have, it's what you do with them that counts. If you have 200 engaged people who follow you, who love your stuff, who interact with you and buy from you, this is better than having 5000 people who have no idea who you are.

If you already have your Facebook page up and running, focus on adding value to the audience you have. If you haven't got it up and running you could do a targeted advertising campaign to grow the number of people who 'like' your page. However, if you're going to be paying for this, look to stop that campaign when you hit 500 likes.

The next thing that you can do is run a targeted advertising campaign where you give away a free resource that will help solve a problem that your audience has. For example, I give away a *Free 30 Day Journaling Series*. All someone needs to do is provide me with their best email address and I send it through to them. Sending out free stuff not only builds your email database so you can communicate with your audience outside of social media, it also has people liking your page as well, so your audience numbers grow in two ways.

6. Do I need to do live videos (live streams)?

Yes, if you can, please do them! People love them. Videos get more free, organic reach so go for it! They don't need to be long (like the blogging, they just go for as long as they need). You'll find if they go for at least 10 minutes, you'll get a second round of fresh viewers on the video while you're live. Follow the blogging/vlogging structure to start with!

INSTAGRAM

Instagram is a great platform for you if you have a lot of visual content or if you know your hot coal clients hang out on there often. You can grow your presence and profile on Instagram *in addition to Facebook*. If your audience isn't on there, then don't invest your time in being present on Instagram.

Instagram FAQs

1. Do I have to create a business, creator or personal account on Instagram?

If you're going to use Instagram to grow your business following, then you've got to set up a business account. You receive better metrics with a business account and data you can drill down into to learn about your audience and their behaviours.

Creator accounts are designed for high-profile users who need to tap deeper into their data. They're also set up for brand management.

2. Do I have to post 'stories' online?

Stories are the pictures that people put up in their apps that only last for 24 hours. I would recommend posting stories.

WHERE ROCK STARS HANG OUT

They are quick, short, sharp and shiny screen grabs (great for the visual people). They are excellent for Influence types who often have shorter attention spans!

3. Do I put photos up? Food photos? What kind of photos? (And does anyone really care what I had for lunch?)

Well, Instagram only lets you put up images. You can use photos taken on your smartphone or you can create picture quotes with text on them and share those (more on that in chapter 8). And, yes, your people do care about what you had for lunch! It helps them get a 'behind the scenes' look at you and, who knows, maybe that kale salad (or meat pie) could be the very thing that sparks conversation!

4. Should I be using InstagramTV (IGTV)?

If you can, absolutely. You can use the blogging/vlogging advice I gave you earlier. A great thing about IGTV is you can upload a video that you have already created. It doesn't need to be 'live'. (More on that in chapter 9, when I talk about how to re-use some of your content rather than constantly creating new content for each platform.)

LINKEDIN

LinkedIn is great if you have more of a professional clientele, or if you know that they spend their time on LinkedIn. People tend to spend approximately ten minutes a day on LinkedIn. It's more of a 'get in and get out' type of platform, rather than a browsing platform.

LinkedIn FAQs

1. How often should I post on LinkedIn?

As with all platforms, I recommend you post daily. You might post slightly less frequently on LinkedIn, but you still need to show up in the newsfeed. Aim for at least one post per day and increase your output from there.

2. How long should my posts be?

Posts on LinkedIn have a character limit so they may need to be shorter than your Facebook posts. Follow the blogging/ vlogging formula and make it shorter and punchier for this platform.

3. Should I use video?

All social media platforms are loving video and rewarding users who post video content. Like IGTV, you don't have to be 'live' on LinkedIn if you don't want to be, it's completely up to you. (More on that in chapter 9.)

NOW IT'S TIME TO DO IT!

Now you know the three places online that are the most populated and the most leverageable:

1. You've got your website.

2. You'll have a Facebook business profile.

3. You'll choose between Instagram and LinkedIn for your second platform.

That's it in terms of platforms. There are, of course, many others (as mentioned earlier), however, these three will give you the fastest traction.

What should I put on these platforms?

I want you to own the fact that you are adding value for your audience with every piece of content you put up online. From the seemingly inconsequential things (like posting about how you work out in the morning or a photo of your morning coffee while journaling) through to more detailed blogs and posts where you might step your audience though the 'three things they can do right now to save money', every post you put up is adding value.

I call this 'value stacking' and it becomes a bit like a game. For every piece of value you post, you get one value stacking point. For every five value stacking points, you earn the right to ask your audience to do something. You could put up a post selling something. You might ask them to opt in for a free training session that you're running. Or you could even invite them to send you their details so you can run through a free discovery session with them. This is how we start to get a return on investment for all the effort we've been putting in.

The types of posts you can put up include:

- Text posts (think back to your IP that you created and come up with one thing that you could say about one of the points in there)
- Lifestyle photos
- An excerpt from a blog
- A live stream
- A picture quote/meme with a motivational/inspirational message

- A video that someone else has created
- An article that you've written
- A photo of you with text in the post.

You are only limited by your imagination.

If you aim for five posts per day, it means you earn the right with your five value stacking points to have one post every day going up specifically offering something for sale (or offering a discovery session, etc.).

I strongly recommend scheduling in advance the picture quote/meme types of posts. You could have two per day. Schedule a text motivational post to go up once per day. Then you only have to do two posts per day that are 'on the fly' or 'in the moment'.

You've got this! You can do it! Start small and work your way up.

This is the price you pay for stepping into the spotlight.

Remember you need to do the work

The benefit of doing all of this work is that you will be visible. You will be in the spotlight. You will be seen and known, recognised and followed. This flow on will get you more clients. You will become known as an expert in your industry.

But you need to do <u>all the activities</u> outlined in this book and, remember, you are freaking awesome!

CHAPTER SUMMARY

DOWNLOAD THE IP WORKSHEET FROM MY WEBSITE AND CREATE:

- IP PART 1 – THE BIG 4
- IP PART 2 – THE 3 PIECES THAT MAKE UP EACH PIECE OF THE BIG 4
- IP PART 3 – 4 ACTIVITIES/CONCEPTS THAT HELP FACILITATE/TEACH/EDUCATE/CREATE EACH OF THE 3 PIECES FROM PART 2
- IP PART 4 – THREATS
- IP PART 5 – DATA/CASE STUDIES/STORIES.

DECIDE WHAT PLATFORMS YOU NEED TO FOCUS ON.

LEARN TO VALUE STACK.

EIGHT
EXPANDING YOUR INFLUENCE

IN 1974 AND 1975, my parents both came separately from the UK, with their families, to live in Australia. My parents were 16 and 17 at the time – I can't even fathom a move that big at that age. I have three children and I can't imagine moving interstate with them, let alone moving internationally! My parents met within the first year of the move and connected through music. They used to go to the local soccer club to hang out with other English people, talk and dance to the music played by the DJ.

Music was a very big part of the youth culture in the UK (and Australia) and having a place where they could go that felt 'normal', even for a while – a place filled with other English people new to Australia – made it feel a bit more like home for them.

My parents met in Adelaide at the iconic Allans music store, where they were both poring over records. They hit it off! Dad had been doing gigs as a DJ before he met my mum. Naturally, given that Mum too was very much into music, when they began dating, they decided to start DJ-ing together. They bought all the equipment, and already had the records and a bit of sass (now you know where I get it from!). They immersed themselves in the music.

Mum was DJ-ing with Dad around Adelaide up until she was about eight months' pregnant with me. So, music has been a big part of my world since before I was even born. My parents each had other jobs. Dad worked as a metal worker and Mum worked for the government as an administration clerk. DJ-ing was their side hustle. They loved music so much, and loved dancing and being able to move the crowd, that they couldn't *not* do it! What a side hustle they had!

After I was born it got a bit tougher, and I became their side hustle! (Not really; naturally, I was the main event!) They sold their much-loved equipment and turned their focus to growing me into the fabulous human I am today. (Haha, did you like that, parents?)

What I loved about growing up, and I'm sure this will resonate with many of you, was the music channel on television which we had on every Saturday morning, as we cleaned up, dancing about doing the housework.

I learned to play the violin and the clarinet (as well as the mandatory primary school recorder). I fell in love with music – all kinds of music. When we went to visit my grandparents, my favourite thing to do was to go into the back room, turn on the organ and teach myself as best I could how to plug away at the keyboard. It felt like music was part of my soul. Singing, playing music or listening to it – I loved it.

In around 1992 to 1993, I remember being at my grandparents' house and my aunty was putting an album on the record player. There were so many records to look through and choose from. I can still smell the smell and feel the texture of the cardboard sleeves that the records used to sit in. There's nothing quite like trying to get a vinyl record in or out of those sleeves without scratching it! The children of today have no idea.

The album my aunty was playing was Queen's 'Greatest Hits'. I knew some of the words because Mum and Dad used to play their music at home. I was 'wowed' with the whole album. I loved the music. I loved the beat. I was a Queen tragic from that moment on! What's strange about that is I knew some of the songs, but listening to the whole album, with all of their hits, did something to me that I had never experienced before then. I was hooked!

I'd play music when I was cleaning up the yard where I kept my horse. I'd take my radio and cassette player combo down to the back of the property so I could perform to the crops over the back fence. Music, the singers, the artists, the bands – they all made me feel as if I wasn't alone. I remember at night, armed with a torch and notebook, I'd listen to the Top 10 countdown on the radio and document it! I thought one day it might be helpful.

You see, music and musicians have the divine gift of being able to heal with their music; to inspire with their music; to influence with their music. What's more, they can use their platform, their positioning and their fame to talk about the things that are important to them.

> **Music moves people, because it creates a connection between the music, the melody and the mindset of the audience. It brings people together. Your content, your message and *you* being in the spotlight will do this, too.**

You only have to think back to the music benefit concert, Fire Fight Australia, which was put on in 2020 after Australia's devastating bushfires. It raised $9.5 million! Queen + Adam Lambert happened to be in Australia at the time, and they took to the stage at the benefit and played their set from Live Aid. It was the first time they had played live since 1985. In addition to the performances on stage, hundreds of celebrities donated money rather than their time.

Musicians, rock stars, bands and performers use their influence all the time to get people to buy their music. It's why there are still, to this day, music channels dedicated solely to playing new music, old music, country music – all kinds of music. We see music clips that are made like mini movies, taking the viewer on a journey through the artistic mind of the creator, influencing us to listen, sing and dance to their songs. The ultimate goal, of course, is that the viewer will buy the single, purchase the album, buy the concert tickets when they're released, and then buy the merchandise that will inevitably be on sale at the concert.

BUILD A TRIBE

It's not just musicians who can create this influence. You too can do this, starting by creating a movement that brings together like-minded people – a community that shares similar tastes. Seth Godin calls it 'tribe building'. He writes: *'A tribe is a group of people connected to one another, connected to a leader, and connected to an idea'*. This is what you're doing: bringing people together, connecting them, leading them and helping them. You can have this influence. You can become the rock star of your industry.

You have everything you need to do this right now, in your hot little hands.

You can use your influence for anything that is important to you.

Take a client of mine, Joanne, for example. Joanne is a music teacher who teaches children and adults how to play the piano – using unconventional methods. There's no smacking of the wrists for her students if they stuff things up! And, for a while, they don't even have to try to make sense of the black dots dancing about on the lines on the white paper. She has a great way of teaching music. I've heard the most amazing stories of children who have loved their musical experience learning in this way. There is something else in Joanne's world, though, that she is passionate about – the adoption process in Australia. She doesn't agree with it as it stands right now. She doesn't agree with the way that birth certificates are changed and a whole lineage and history is deleted from a human, essentially without their consent because, of course, most adoptions are completed when children are little.

Joanne uses her platform every now and then to share her thoughts about adoption. She educates her audience on things that are important to her – in addition to teaching them piano. She's had many people come back to her exclaiming that they didn't know or fully understand what the process was like and how much it can impact someone as an adult – even when they had a relatively 'normal' upbringing with their adoptive families.

This is where influence can come in. You can use your influence within the scope of your business to get your audience to join you on tour, buy your books and listen to your podcasts. Then you can invite them to share these things with the people they know! This is where the tribe effect kicks in. We see it happen on social media all the time, when something someone says resonates with people and they share it far and wide. Of course, you can also use your influence, like Joanne does, to educate people on additional issues, causes and ideas that are important to you.

The more connected you are to your audience, the more you actually know them, the easier it is to influence them.

In fact, chances are, they already share your values and when they hear you talk about the things that are important to you, they're likely to listen.

Think of this as building a friendship. The more you get to know someone (and like them), the more you enjoy spending time with them. When they then invite you to go a concert with them, you're more likely to say *hell yes!*

Influence is important, because people are looking for leaders. They're looking for people they can trust. Your audience is looking for people to follow, learn from and buy from, who remind them of themselves in some way.

By growing influence, you build a platform to take your business, your marketing, your services to the next level. Many clients of mine tell me that they want to do world tours. They want to put on life-changing conferences that aren't boring! Where every single person in the room achieves massive breakthroughs, ah-ha moments and insights that will help them to make changes for the better.

This is the next level, the next stage, the global version of you. People will be talking about *you*, some 20 or more years after working with you or attending an event of yours that they recollect fondly.

A WORD OF CAUTION

When you've got your plan and strategy (which you have, because you've done *all* of the activities up this point, right?), and you're implementing it, there are some things that can happen.

One issue people can run into is when they get very excited about making everything happen and they start to see amazing results. They feel confident. Their energy is where they need it to be. They are *bringing it*, so to speak. Then they get a bit bored with the level that they're playing at. They want a new challenge. They want to reach a new audience. They want something that's going to push them up a gear, give them that extra drive, to really go big into the stratosphere.

Then they hit their upper limits when it comes to their capacity to expand and take on the world. An upper limit is like the glass ceiling that we impose consciously or unconsciously on ourselves.

I've seen people burn out. I've seen people blow up their businesses and burn them to the ground, so that they have the thrill of building and creating something new again.

Now, this is not the most resourceful way of finding a thrill, is it? No! There are far too many people out there who need you. There are many people who want to be in your stadiums. There are many people out there who want to read your books. There are people out there who want *you*.

Let's make it happen.

THE THREE STAGES TO BUILDING INFLUENCE

It's not enough to just put some posts up on social media and show up now and again. You've got an audience to find, build and grow. There are three steps to go through to leverage everything you have at this point if you want to create fame, influence and impact.

The three stages we're going to work through together in this chapter are:

Expansion | Certainty | Leverage

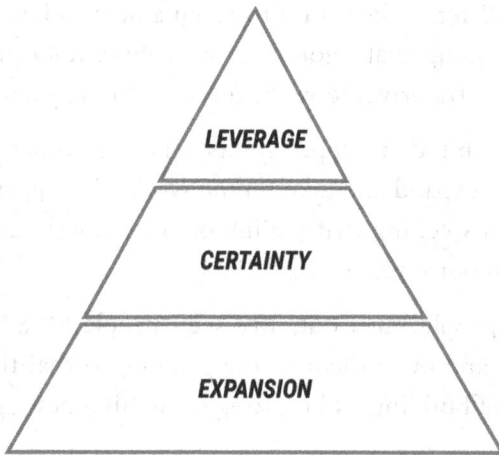

LEVERAGE

CERTAINTY

EXPANSION

Expansion

By the time you get to this stage of being in the spotlight, you'll have your hot coal clients and you'll be thoroughly loving working with them. You've mastered what you're doing so well that you could probably do it with your eyes closed, one arm tied behind your back and tied to a chair! You're unconsciously competent at what you do and how you do it.

Honestly, this can sometimes feel a little, well, boring. You no longer have the thrill of reaching 'the first $100K' or 'the first million'. You don't have the excitement of the *'Oh my gosh, I have to put out a video!'* moments and the adrenalin hit that comes with that. You might start wondering, *'Is this as good as it gets?'* I've been there. I've felt that and it sucks. You know that you have done great things and you want more, but it can be challenging at times to find the next thing, that next goal or the next challenge.

So, here it is; this is your next challenge:

Your next challenge is to become iconic, to become legendary.

The Genius Loop

About seven years into my business, I remember having a chat with one of my besties (Jo Muirhead – follow her online, she's a total bad-ass!) who I've been friends with since 2011 when we were on a retreat together with a mentor we shared. I was telling her I had an itch, a really bad business itch. I wanted more and I couldn't work out how to make it happen.

'Back then' I was teaching people how to create online marketing systems focused in large part around the technology that they needed to use to get their funnels built, their online forms created and what to do with their audiences from there. There was a heavy focus on how to use Facebook to grow your business. It's still part of what I do today but, back then, it was the sole focus. You know the saying, *'Sell them what they want and give them what they need'*? That's what I was doing. But it didn't fulfil me.

I was very well known in the industry and with business owners for 'crushing it' in the online space. But I was burned out and wanted to do deeper work – my soul work. I have always wanted to help people create a business and life they love while making a ton of money by helping other people. I wanted to only work with people I liked and who I'd love to hang out with. People who were of similar mind to me and radically fun to be around.

Jo came to visit me at my home (yes, she travelled all the way to Mildura!) and, while she was here, I created the Genius Loop. It was a model that described my journey and one that I'd noticed in other people. It showed the shedding of old ways that no longer worked and helped me to step into the work that I wanted to do.

The Genius Loop

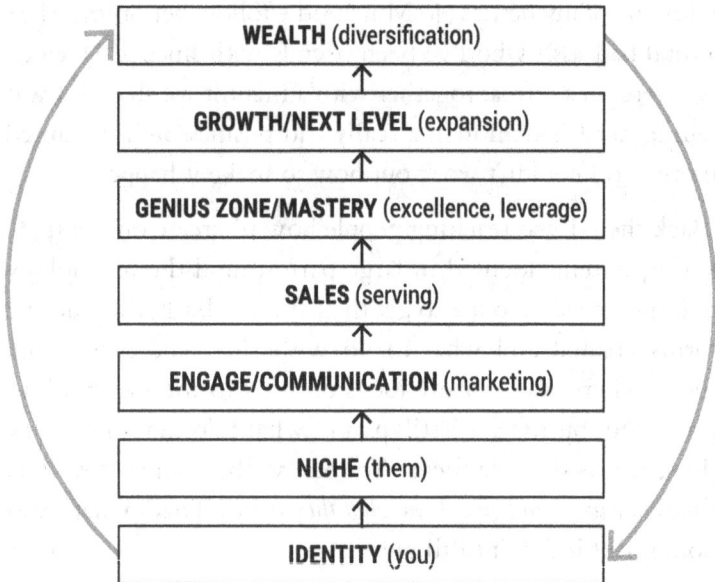

When you've mastered your craft and things are going along beautifully, it becomes time for you to step into the next level of you, the next growth phase. You reinvent your goals, your plans and the way you do things. When you step into the growth/next level phase (see above), you have reached a new level of 'you-ness' that needs to be brought out into the world.

Completing the Genius Loop will renew your commitment to expansion.

✳ ACTIVITY: Dream big

Here's what I want you to do. Sit down and do some work on what you really want, more than anything, for your business. Imagine what you would want if there were no barriers, no boundaries and no 'realistic' expectations.

- Do you want to write books and get paid for it?

- What about touring the world, speaking to stadiums filled with audiences who are all there for you?

- What does the next level look like?

- Do you want to live off the grid?

- What about designing wearable art and selling it around the world?

- Maybe it's about expanding into new regions or developing new products and services.

- The sky really is the limit! Dream big.

It's in this stage of stepping into the spotlight when you double down on your dreams and your desires and you decide to give it your all. I mean, isn't building a business all about having the freedom and choice to live your life the way you want, as well as running your business the way you want?

What you need to create at this point is a version 2.0 of you, the rock star. I want you to consider what someone who has all of this already looks like, talks about and sounds like. How do they dress? What do they know? What do you need to learn to step it up? And who are you going to learn from to make all of this happen?

I remember in 2019, I was doing a national tour for an event I was running, and I was walking along the river in Perth before the day got underway. I was listening to music, bobbing along on my merry way, keeping a pretty fast pace. Then, all of a sudden, I could see the vision that I wanted for my business and *how* I was going to take it there. I could see the way it would be run, who would be in it with me, the faces of the people who would be clients. It was crystal clear and so specific. I was blown away. It had taken a long time for me to reach that point of seeing in my head the way it could actually happen. I'd had dreams for years about where I wanted to take my business, but I couldn't see *how* I was going to do that until I had that vision. I got so excited about it, I dropped a very long voice message to Jo and shared my vision with her. It felt aligned, exciting and expansive.

I had given myself permission to dream bigger, to think bigger than I'd ever done before – and the vision landed itself in my lap. It was then that I knew that I had to start working on bringing that to life.

Certainty

Along the way, it's easy to stumble and get caught up in the day-to-day drama and leg-work of building your business and tending to your clients – and you start to forget your awesomeness. It can be tough to maintain your inner confidence when you're branching back out again. Sometimes the allure of staying in the same place that you're in right now, and doing the same things you've always been doing, can feel safe and secure – a bit like your favourite hoodie. But we all know that this is not going to get you to where you really want to be.

You need to activate your inner certainty.

I have run events for years in person as well as online; big events and very intimate events. I still remember the very first big event that I put on in 2013. I was so scared! I was super-nervous and worried primarily that I would forget my words, or worse, run out of things to say! Can you imagine? I know! Yet, there I was, prepping for this event, running every scenario through my head about what could possibly happen.

You see, I had never done this before. I didn't know what I was doing. I had a mentor who I was working with who helped me immensely with the producing of the event but, for me, it was still the first time and there were so many unknowns. I had Jo as my Mistress of Ceremonies for the event and she was getting the crowd warmed up for me. I remember standing at the back of the function room that led into the kitchen area, waiting to be introduced, feeling so excited and, yes, nervous, to get out there and help my people.

The second that door opened, and I danced through the middle of the audience making my way up the stairs to the stage, I knew that it would all be okay. It would be amazing. And, of course, it was. That event changed many lives including my own.

As a result of planning something I'd never done before, I found a sense of certainty that I could make anything in this business work. I would find the words. I would be able to deliver exactly what I needed to in order to create the results that my people wanted – and needed.

It helped me to find my voice.

You see, at this stage in your business growth, you really have to dispense with the idea that everyone has to like you. I know, I know. It can be a tough pill to swallow. Yet, it's also a necessary pill. If you're going to step things up a notch, you need to find this inner confidence and certainty that comes from throwing yourself off at the deep end.

Think back to when you first started your business. Perhaps you were a little like I was. I used to think, *'Well, if it doesn't work, that's okay! I'll just go and get a job or beg for my old job back! It'll be fine'*. Whereas when you're in this next phase of growth, it can feel like you've got a lot more to lose and so many tend to play it safe.

You need to find *your* voice. You need to remember and acknowledge that you have come so freaking far and that you have helped many people up to this point. Remind yourself that you have everything to gain.

How do you do that? Well, you need to look back at all the evidence of what you've achieved and don't downplay it. Growing your business can be a little like childbirth: you somehow forget the pain until you really take the time to remember all the details.

Remind yourself every single day that you've got this.

Who has your back?

Often, it's not enough to be your own cheer squad when you're embarking on this next phase of growth. You need people in your world who have your back, because sometimes it's hard to remember your own amazingness.

I love how Janine Garner talks about this in her book *It's Who You Know*. She says, *'Start with 4 and aim for 12'* people in your network. She outlines four categories:

1. Teachers
2. Promoters
3. Pit crew
4. Butt-kickers.

In each of these categories, you need someone to have your back. You don't have to be paying them mentoring or coaching fees – although I always recommend having at least one mentor on your team (they can be a friend or a peer). The guidelines are simple, though. They have to have your back.

The good thing about this is that you have four other people reminding you that you're awesome! You have a teacher who reminds you that you already know a lot – and there's more to learn. You have a promoter who talks about you to their networks and communities and who, in turn, reminds you of your awesomeness. You have someone in your pit crew who is like the person who 'gets' you more than anyone else does and sees your awesomeness and reminds you of it. And you have your butt-kicker, who is someone who kicks your ass any time you need it, reminding you that you've got this and you can do it.

It's important to note that you're not trying to get your support people to 'like you' any more than they already do. You don't need them to approve of what you're doing or to validate you. These people form your sounding board, your advisory board.

They are people you trust to tell you the truth, kick your ass and listen to you without judgement. They'll give you suggestions, feedback, ideas and thoughts that will benefit you.

This kind of external validation is very different to getting people to like you. They will cheer you on, they will support you, but they will not blow hot air up your hoo-hah just to make sure that you don't get upset. Additionally, they won't hold back when something is amazing.

Certainty comes from within, but who honestly doesn't also love a bit of external validation?

Leveraging your performance

Before they get to this point, many people have experienced some form of burnout. Perhaps they were burning the candle at both ends trying to get their businesses up and running, or maybe it came from working with clients or doing work that they didn't love.

This is not sustainable. If you want to reach new heights and hit the new goals that you've established for yourself, you've honestly got to make sure that you're managing your 'wheel of life' for peak performance.

Wheel of life

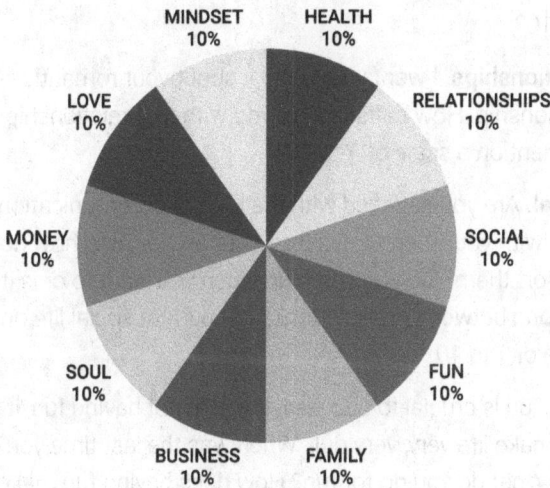

As you can see in the diagram, there are ten segments in your wheel of life:

1. Health
2. Relationships
3. Social
4. Fun
5. Family

6. Business
7. Soul
8. Money
9. Love
10. Mindset.

Let's do an activity to see where you are at each stage of the wheel of life.

✳ ACTIVITY: Where are you on the wheel of life?

1. **Health.** Health is your physical health, as well as your mental and emotional health. If your physical body is not how you want it to be in order for it to do the things you will need it to do while you continue to grow into the rock star you are (and are becoming), then where would you rank that on a scale of 1 to 10?

2. **Relationships.** I want you to think about your romantic relationship. How satisfied are you with that relationship at the moment on a scale of 1 to 10?

3. **Social.** Are you satisfied with the level of communication you have with your friends? Do they support you, and how do you support them? Do you catch up when you want to or is it far too long between drinks? Rank your current social life on a scale of 1 to 10.

4. **Fun.** Fun is crucial to success. If you're not having fun, it really can make life very, very dull. When was the last time you had fun? What do you do for fun? How does having fun make you feel? Rank your current satisfaction level about how you 'do' fun on a scale of 1 to 10.

5. **Family.** Family is your immediate family and your extended family. How satisfied are you with the relationships that you have with each family member? Are you happy with the way things are or can you see room for improvement? Remember that different family members might have different relationships with you, and that's okay. You may see some more than others or talk more with some than others. There is no right or wrong with them, it's about how satisfied *you* are. Rank your satisfaction from 1 to 10.

6. **Soul.** Your connection to your soul, source, spirit, universe, god, energy, your higher self, the divine is important when it comes to reaching new heights. It's also been heavily documented that it's crucial to feel as if you're part of a bigger picture. How is this showing up in your world at the moment and how happy are you with your connection? Rank this from 1 to 10.

7. **Business.** Some people rank their business low because they feel like they need to improve. They may feel they need to make more money before ranking this a 7 or an 8 out of 10. They might be happy with the way things are going but fear that, if they 'settle', they won't grow.

    This is not necessarily true for many people. You can still be happy with everything in your business but want to make more money. You might then rank your satisfaction at a 6 out of 10. Where is it for you?

8. **Money.** Many people may feel very grateful that they are making the money and might feel it's a bit like a slap in the face to say *'it's not enough'*. Or, conversely, they may have a lot of money and don't feel like they need to make more. It doesn't matter where you are at. You just need to rank on a scale of 1 to 10 how satisfied you are with your financial situation.

9. **Love.** How loved do you feel right now, overall, on a scale of 1 to 10? This is the combination of feeling loved and loving those around you.

10. **Mindset.** How is your mindset right now? Are you a 'cup half full' person and generally positive, or not? Do you have a growth mindset or a fixed mindset? Do you believe that you can achieve what you want to achieve in life or that you are a victim of circumstance? Rank how happy you are overall with your mindset on a scale of 1 to 10.

In order to be in a peak performance state, most of us don't need to be a 10 in all of the above areas. But we need to have things at least at a 7 or 8 across most for us to feel like we're successful, happy and reasonably well balanced.

For instance, if you've been super-focused on building and growing your business, perhaps you've let the satisfaction with your health drop to a 3 out of 10 and you want it to be a 7 or 8? You might need to join a gym or sign up for an online exercise program. Hustle up your advisory board and have them hold you accountable to your goals. (They don't just have to be there to support you with your business!)

To achieve the heights that you want to reach, you've got to be in a peak performance state.

When you have completed the wheel of life activity, you need to take the following steps:

1. Identify where you are on a scale of 1 to 10 in each segment

2. Identify what you need to work on

3. Create an action plan, in each area, of one or two things you can do to move the needle up (even if it's only one notch) on the segments you feel need it

4. Schedule these actions

5. Create accountability by sharing your plan with your support crew

6. Implement the plan

7. Assess its success or what needs to happen/change.

> **Remember, your dreams are worth it. You are worth it. You're a bad-ass.**

Author Gay Hendricks in *The Big Leap* talks about *'the spiral'* and how *'you go higher and higher every day as you expand your capacity for more love, abundance, and success. It's an upward journey with no upper limit'*.

By focusing on your next goal and your next dream, as we have been doing in this chapter, and then taking action on making it happen, you're going to continue to evolve and expand as a business owner and as a human.

The payoff for doing this is the evolution of *you*, your next iteration, which is super-exciting. Additionally, you're going to have the energy to sustain this new level of you and what you want to create.

Most importantly, I think, you're going to be able to build a business that creates a legacy of massive change and influence in other people's lives.

INTERVIEW WITH THE WOLFE BROTHERS

'It was just going to happen no matter what', said Tom of Nick and Tom of Wolfe Brothers fame. The brothers hit our screens in Australia on 'Australia's Got Talent' in 2012, but not before they had years of experience under their belts.

They have performed from a young age, and they both have a different approach to being in the spotlight. Tom is a self-confessed extrovert who thrives on attention, and Nick is often more comfortable doing his thing and doing it well – not being front and centre stage. They both have had to adjust to being in the spotlight in their own ways. They might give what looks like an effortless performance, but there have been things they've needed to refine along the way.

When I interviewed Nick and Tom, as well as being wonderfully generous and gracious with their time and their insights, the big thing that came through was their commitment to their audiences around the world. They are a couple of down-to-earth men, who seem to be deeply in love with their craft and the way they're able to create an experience for their fans.

They shared their journey with me: from gigging around Tasmania four or five nights a week to playing at birthdays and weddings, to finally getting their big break on 'Australia's Got Talent' in 2012 and hitting new goals like touring the US. They had a lot to work through over the years, but they persisted to live the dream.

The advice they wanted to impart to you is this:

- Be you and you own that. People want you to be you. 'There's a lot of people out there doing this sort of thing. And you've got to find your own track. Too many people try to conform to what they think is totally trendy in their genre or their field. Just be you.'

- You've got to get out there and do the good gigs with the bad and the small – and work that combination.

- You're going to get it wrong a few times. And that's okay. You figure it out and you just get up and do it again. Just keep getting back up.

- You've got to do 10,000 hours at something to be good at it.

- Have goals. Achieve them and then set new ones. Always know what you're aiming for, so that if you get lost, you have something to look towards.

CHAPTER SUMMARY

YOU NEED TO BUILD YOUR TRIBE.

THERE ARE THREE STAGES OF INFLUENCE TO WORK THROUGH.

DREAM BIG AND LEVERAGE YOUR PERFORMANCE.

FIND OUT WHO HAS YOUR BACK. WHO'S ON YOUR BIG 4 ADVISORY BOARD?

ASSESS ALL AREAS OF YOUR LIFE BY DOING THE WHEEL OF LIFE ACTIVITY.

CREATE A PLAN TO IMPROVE THE AREAS THAT NEED FURTHER WORK.

NINE
LIGHTS, CAMERA, ACTION

THE STAGE IS SET. The lights are on. You can feel the electricity in the room as you prepare to walk up the steps and onto the stage. You know that nobody else on this planet can walk up there for you. Nobody can do the work that you're about to do. Not one other human on the planet is you, or even like you. You are the only one who knows the entire performance, the entire event – everything is up to you.

You've got the most amazing support team: your cheer squad, your pit crew and your butt-kicker. You've got the presence, the platform and you've been putting yourself out there. You know exactly who your hot coal clients are – and they're all waiting out there for you. You know your zone of awesomeness, you know your strengths and you've got your mindset nailed.

All that's left for you to do is rock the house and, dammit, that's what you're going to do!

You've got to take action!

I remember the main character in Paulo Coelho's *The Alchemist* talking about finding his treasure. He often got 'sidetracked' on his journey to finding his hidden treasure, but he kept on taking action after action that eventually got him there. The path was long, windy and convoluted. There were dramas and speedbumps along the way, times when he lost everything and times when he felt he had it all. He kept coming back to his dream, though. He kept taking action without really knowing where he was going or which roads he should take. He just kept taking one consistent action after another, after another.

Your dream goal is your treasure. Your dream goal is something that you have decided to take action on and make happen.

All that's left now is for you to do it (if you haven't already) and keep doing it. As the Pantene ad says, *'It won't happen overnight, but it will happen'*.

Think of all the action you've taken already as like building a snowball. Every time you take action, that snowball gets bigger and bigger. The bigger it gets, the faster it rolls down the mountain, gathering speed, getting bigger and bigger and bigger.

This is what stepping into the spotlight does when you do it over and over again.

I can promise you this: you can do this. You must do this. Now, you need to make it happen!

I talk a lot about stepping into the spotlight and making this happen for you, but why? So that you can help more people, which means you're going to get more clients, which means you're going to make more money. It's a simple equation:

You in the spotlight = money.

And when you make money, you have choices. When you're making money consistently, you have more freedom. When you have more freedom, you get to make choices about the kind of lifestyle you want to have.

Entrepreneurs are driven by these three things:

1. Freedom

2. Choice

3. Lifestyle.

You are driven by these three things, otherwise you wouldn't be an entrepreneur or have your own business! You'd be working for someone else, letting someone else deal with the stress of managing cash flow, doing the marketing and everything that goes along with having a business of your own. If it were really only about doing what you love, you'd be working for someone else and you'd just take the pay cheque.

You're doing this because you want to do what you love to do – every single day – *and* create the choice, freedom and lifestyle you desire. You want to build, create and grow a legacy. You want to give freely and generously to causes that you care about; to help out your children and other family members; to spoil your friends without worrying about how you're going to do that. You're doing this for more than just the love of what you do.

The big thing to remember is this: failure is inevitable. You will fail. What matters most is what you do after that.

Let's help you get into action, baby.

First things first, we're going to break this down into some easy things that you can do. After all, the way you eat an elephant is one bite at a time.

PLANNING

I remember hearing a quote, *'if it's not scheduled, it's not going to happen'* and I am a firm believer in this. I like to add, *'if it's not planned, then you don't know what to schedule'*. Think back to the big, huge goals that you had when you were reading earlier on, and how good it felt to sit with those goals, and anticipate achieving them. It felt amazing. I love getting into that space. However, often it can feel as if I'm a long, long way from those ever coming to life.

Here's what you're going to do to drag your goals closer to you.

The next 12 months

What would be a great outcome for you over the next 12 months, if you knew that every single thing you did would take you closer to achieving your big dream? Fast-forward 12 months and imagine that you achieved everything that you wanted to, everything that you said you would achieve. Now, on a piece of paper (or download the worksheet from my website), write down how you're feeling, what you're noticing, what you've done and all of the positive things you've noticed as a result of it.

That's great. Yet, your goal can still a bit far away, can't it? Let's break it down now to something super-achievable.

The next 90 days

If you think about it, 90 days (or 12 weeks) fly by. There's a change of season. Your BAS comes due again – this comes around far too quickly, right? You can achieve a lot in 90 days if you put your mind to it.

When you look at your 12-month goal, imagine that you know exactly what you need to do to achieve that goal. For instance, if your 12-month goal is to finally hit the $100K per year or the $100K per month mark, you might have to get your website updated, write a book, launch your podcast, create a mastermind or even start promoting your courses.

Brainstorm everything that you can do over the next 90 days (you don't need to know how to do these things yet, you just need to have an action plan started) and write these things down under your 12-month achievement.

The next 30 days

Now we're going to get even more specific. Take a look at your 90-day list of things that you can do to take you closer to achieving your 12-month goal and pick what you are going to take action on in the next 30 days. For instance, if you're going to write a book in the next 90 days, within the next 30 days you'll need to write your book plan. If one of your 90-day goals is to be healthy and fit, then in the next 30 days you'll make sure you research gym programs and the equipment you'll need.

It might feel like you now have a laundry list of things to do and that's okay. We're going to break it down even further.

The next week

This is where things start to get fun! You're going to need to be very specific in this section, as this will determine how your week is planned out. Look at the 30-day list of what you're going to do, and break this down even further into which week of the month you're going to do those tasks in.

For instance, if you had *'create a podcast'* as one of your action items, in week 1 of the month you might research the software needed to do this. You'd probably order any equipment you may need. In week 2, you might spend time brainstorming all your content that you'll share on the podcast. Week 3 would be for podcast creation and week 4 for podcast editing.

By doing this, you're creating smaller and smaller specific, actionable items that you know you'll be able to make progress on, easily.

Each day, Monday to Friday

Now that you have your week 1 list ready to go, you need to break these tasks down into smaller actions and allocate them to a day of the week.

For instance, in the podcast example, on Monday you might download software. On Tuesday you could research the equipment needed; Wednesday's when you find music for the introduction; on Thursday you brainstorm taglines and Friday's when you create a podcast cover.

This is the part of your planning when the actions get actioned. You now have your list of what to do each day of this week.

What's stopping you? That's right! *Nothing.*

SCHEDULE IT

The most important thing you can do while you're building your online presence and stepping into the spotlight is *to actually do it.* Unfortunately, all the planning in the world doesn't make that happen on its own. (I know, we all feel a little ripped off by that one!) The good news is that there is a way that you *can* make it happen, and that involves you being proactive in implementing your plan.

Many people need to build the muscle of online visibility, and it can feel a bit scary at first. There are a zillion and one things that you need to do on top of this; I get it. You need to get these things scheduled in.

Some people like the idea of having a fluid day, where they deal with what comes up as it comes up. They will wait for the 'mood' to strike them before getting into their tasks, and they select the tasks they'll do based on how they feel. This doesn't work for most people. In fact, I'd say that it works for hardly anyone in the process of building muscle.

Let's imagine you decide you want to enter a weightlifting competition so you go the gym and you map out everything the way that you've learned here. You know it's going to take 12 months to be strong and fit enough; you've got a focus for the next 90 days, the next 30 days, then tasks each week and each day. On the list is: *'go to the gym and lift some weights'*. On Monday, you're excited and motivated and so you go. On Tuesday, though, you're a little sore and you're waiting to 'feel like' going to the gym. It doesn't happen. Wednesday rolls around and it's the same. Thursday rolls around and you feel an inkling of motivation and you head there. Friday you're not feeling it. If this pattern continues, there is no way that you're going to get to where you want to be. You've failed before you've even started.

Whereas if you have a time set in your schedule for a daily 7am gym visit, and you decide that it's not negotiable to wimp out, you know you must. After a month of continuously showing up at the gym, it starts to get more familiar. The self talk about not going seems to almost disappear, because going to the gym becomes routine. It becomes part of what you do.

It's the same for your online visibility efforts. You want to feel as if they are familiar, safe and part of you – so much so, that if there's a day that you don't do something, *that* feels weird and odd – like you've forgotten to put on one of your shoes before walking out of the door.

Schedule in the key things that you know you need to do and they become the rocks in your schedule.

To start with, I'd recommend doing tasks at the same time on the same day, daily.

Suggested rock-in-the-diary scheduling

9am	Live stream
9.30am–10am	Schedule your social media posts for the day = *rock in the diary*
10am–10.15am	Email your live stream and your latest blog and anything else you want to send to your email list = *rock in the diary*
10am–3pm	Clients, delivery, etc. = *rock in the diary*
3pm–4pm	Pick up children from school = *rock in the diary*
4pm–5.30pm	Clients, wrap up, schedule anything for in the morning = *rock in the diary*

Batching

You can't always do the suggested scheduling on a daily basis. I get it. For the short term, though, I'd like you to give it a go. One of the big things that you must do *each and every day* is put your content out there so that people know that your spotlight is on and you are stepping into it.

In chapter 7, we discussed the importance of value stacking. *(Flash reminder: with every piece of value you put out there, you get one 'value stacking point'. For every five value stacking points you accumulate you can ask your audience to do something.)*

It's super-easy for your day to get hijacked by children, clients, animals, phone calls – the shiny things – and you can find yourself at the end of the day with none of your value stacking done. This sucks, because there's another day that you haven't been able to help a wider audience get to know you.

I had a personal assistant, Bev, for a long time, when my children were younger. I was on sales calls literally all day, every day (which I wouldn't recommend for an extended period of time), and I found it hard to get things done. Bev doubled as a nanny and as my 'home helper'. She'd cook our dinners for us, collect the children from school, run errands for me and essentially she'd make sure that I was eating and that the house wasn't a total disaster zone on a daily basis. She was an angel. I honestly don't know how I would have got through everything without her. By having her here, I was able to find 10 to 12 hours of *productive, essentially billable time* each week, so it made sense. I knew that so long as I made one more sale each week, her wage was covered, I had more time and things would be amazing. They were.

Until she fell in love with a man who lived in another town and she left us for him. #Heartbroken.

When Bev left, I knew that I had to find a way to get everything done, which included cooking dinners in advance otherwise we wouldn't eat until 7.30 or 8 o'clock (which was just not an option when I wanted the kids in bed by 8)! We started batch cooking every second Sunday, when we'd cook on average 10 meals that would see us through most of the upcoming fortnight. It worked like a dream. Dinner would end up late, but not as late. There was less stress and pressure on me to get out of the office and into the kitchen on a daily basis. Batching worked like a dream.

I use the same batching technique, to this day, with some of my social media visibility posts.

We all love seeing motivational quotes on the internet. We all love feeling inspired, the rush of *'Yes, okay, I'm just going to grab life by the short and curlies and I'm going to go and do that thing!'* I want you to be that source of inspiration for your audience. If you have two motivational quote designs and you are posting two each day, there are two value stacking points sitting there waiting to be banked. I have two designs:

1. A numbered series called *'Right between the eyes'*

2. A general series featuring photos of me.

I create 30 *Right between the eyes* posts in advance and another 30 more generic ones. I use the design platform, Canva, and I create 30 because that's the maximum number it allows per design. Thirty is also a good number because it's a month's content in advance in one file.

It shouldn't take you too long to create 30 posts in advance, once you have a template set up. Create something that looks good to you, which ideally has a common thread through-out all of them (like your face on them!) and another that is similar but that perhaps doesn't have your face on them.

Once you have created these, it's a matter of scheduling them. This should only take you somewhere between one and two hours per month. That's two posts scheduled per day – done – and you only need to repeat it monthly!

Block out two hours in your schedule and get it done. Then it's done for a whole month. Later, in about the third week of each month, repeat it for the upcoming month.

This gets your skeleton content up on your social media pro-files, so if you happen to have a day when you don't show up 'live' on the platform, you have still delivered value to your audience.

> **Hint:** You can quote someone else on your posts, just make sure you attribute the quote to them.

> **Bigger hint:** If you have an overarching theme that brings in some fun and drama to your branding, find people to quote who align with that. For instance, I use a lot of music metaphors in my social media, so I will often quote Freddie Mercury, Gwen Stefani and Robbie Williams, for instance.

CREATE YOUR CONTENT MAP

My clients and I are huge fans of visual prompts and remind-ers. If you have a big, visual prompt pinned to your wall or sitting on your desk, you are more likely to take the action, because you're constantly being reminded of it.

You've already done the work! It's now time to get into your content map and use it. Print it off, hang it up on your wall and make it happen.

In chapter 6, we discussed the four phases that you take your audience through that help them achieve the transformation that you provide. Each of these four phases can be your focus for each quarter's content:

- Phase 1 = Quarter 1

- Phase 2 = Quarter 2

- Phase 3 = Quarter 3

- Phase 4 = Quarter 4.

From there, you delved into the three core concepts that you need to talk about so that your audience achieves the phase. These can become the focus for each month within the quarter:

- Quarter 1 = Month 1 concept 1, Month 2 concept 2, Month 3 concept 3, and so on.

Then, I had you brainstorm the four main activities that you will do with your audience to help them achieve those particular goals. These now become the focus for the weeks within each month:

- Month 1 = Week 1 Idea 1, Week 2 Idea 2, Week 3 Idea 3, Week 4 Idea 4.

From there, I am certain that there are at least five different things that you can talk about relevant to each idea. These are five days' worth of ideas that you can share online.

My quarterly content map

Phase 1 for me is **confidence**.

The three concepts that make that up are **mindset**, **knowledge** and **strengths**.

The Month 1 focus for me is **mindset**.

I have four ways of helping people work on their mindset (at least), which form the focus of the content for week 1, week 2, week 3 and week 4.

Week 1 can be on **self-sabotage**. I know of at least five different ways, stories, activities that I can talk about daily to help people past self-sabotage.

DAILY VISIBILITY CHECKLIST

I love how Tony Robbins says, *'Where focus goes, energy flows'*, and that's exactly what needs to happen with your daily visibility: you need to focus. FOCUS is an acronym cleverly designed to remind you what to focus in!

F – Facebook first

You do this first, because Facebook has the biggest audience *and* people spend more than four times the amount of time on Facebook as they do on any other platform.

O – Other platforms

Once you have Facebook done, head over and work on the other platforms.

C – Communicate with them

If you have people commenting on your posts, make sure you reply to them *personally* in the comments. Do not have someone else do it. You're building trust with your audience, and if you've got someone else pretending to be you, well, it's starting the entire relationship off on the wrong foot. You cannot outsource this.

U – Until it's done, don't stop

Sit your butt down. Work through the list of the things that you need to do, and don't stop until it's done. When you set up this level of commitment, you are a lot more likely to get things done, faster.

S – Syndicate it multiple times

Share what you've created and posted multiple times. There are no rules that say you can't re-post the content you've put out there more than once. In fact, I'd recommend it. (There's more coming up in a couple of pages on re-using your content.)

When you do this, you will have more energy flowing through to your online visibility efforts. #Winning.

Daily to-do list

In an ideal world, here's what you need to do daily (remember to work up to it):

- 10 x messaging (sharing your thinking). This means value-adding posts that don't necessarily have a call to action attached to them.

- Sales offer/call to action x 2 or more.

Don't flip your lid! I know that sounds like a lot, so let's make it easy for you.

You already know what your goal is — *to value stack so that you become visible to the hot coal clients you want to work with.* Messaging is the key to bringing them in. Knowing your message (which you worked out in chapter 6) and sharing your content with your audience is what keeps you in the spotlight.

The thing you need to be aware of here is that, out of all the people who follow you, most will only see 10 per cent of what you post. Yes, 10 per cent.

If you are posting 10 times per day, most people will see 1 post per day from you in their newsfeed.

I hear you push back: *'ain't nobody got the time (nor the inclination) to be on social media every minute of every day, trying to grow their presence'.* You've got other things to do, I get it. When you're thinking about your 10 messaging pieces of content, it can feel a bit overwhelming. Here's what you can do specifically to make it easy.

INTRODUCING THE CONTENT SPINNER

The content spinner is how you take one piece of content and re-use it or repurpose it over and over again. If you focus on creating one long piece of content each day, you can use this for your messaging efforts multiple times over.

For instance, say you were to write a blog each day that is 700 words long. There will be paragraphs in there that you can take out and perhaps edit slightly to be a standalone post. Here's how it works:

Messaging points

Blog = 1 piece of content
Blog excerpt x 2 = 3 pieces of content
You would share your blog via email = 4 pieces of content

Blog = 1 piece of content
Blog excerpt x 2 = 3 pieces of content
Email = 4 pieces of content
You can also post the blog with an excerpt and a 'read more' link, which gives you another one.

Blog = 1 piece of content
Blog excerpt x 2 = 3 pieces of content
Email = 4 pieces of content
Blog excerpt posted to social media = 5 pieces of content
You have two picture quotes scheduled in (thanks to batching)

Blog = 1 piece of content
Blog excerpt x 2 = 3 pieces of content
Email = 4 pieces of content
Blog excerpt posted to social media = 5 pieces of content
Picture quotes x 2 = 7 pieces of content
You would then share your blog to LinkedIn/Instagram (or both if you're using both)

Blog = 1 piece of content
Blog excerpt x 2 = 3 pieces of content
Email = 4 pieces of content
Blog excerpt posted to social media = 5 pieces of content
Picture quotes x 2 = 7 pieces of content
Share blog to LinkedIn/Instagram = 8 pieces of content

You can then do a live stream on what you talked about in the blog, because some people prefer to listen and watch rather than read.

Blog = 1 piece of content
Blog excerpt x 2 = 3 pieces of content
Email = 4 pieces of content
Blog excerpt posted to social media = 5 pieces of content
Picture quotes x 2 = 7 pieces of content
Share blog to LinkedIn/Instagram = 8 pieces of content
Live stream = 9 pieces of content
You can email your email list with the live stream link and perhaps one of the picture quotes that you shared that day.

Blog = 1 piece of content
Blog excerpt x 2 = 3 pieces of content
Email = 4 pieces of content
Blog excerpt posted to social media = 5 pieces of content
Picture quotes x 2 = 7 pieces of content
Share blog to LinkedIn/Instagram = 8 pieces of content
Live stream = 9 pieces of content
Email live stream and share picture quote = 11 pieces of content.

I have put together a worksheet for you called the Content Spinner that you can download along with the worksheets that go along with this book (see back of the book).

You are only limited by your imagination when it comes to repurposing your content. It's also smart to create picture quotes out of the sentences from your blog. That way, when you're batching, you don't have to sit there scratching your head trying to come up with 30 ideas! You've already done some of the heavy lifting. *Go you!*

CONVERTING SALES

The very obvious payoff to you stepping into the spotlight and owning your online visibility efforts is that you can make money as a result of it. But only if you're letting people know how to buy from you. Remember that people only see 10 per cent of what you post in their newsfeeds. If you're not regularly letting people know how they can buy from you, then perhaps they don't even know that they *can*, which means both they and you miss out.

Ensure that you have at least two specific sales-driven posts going up each day, while you are in a launch period for your offer or your program. Combined with the messaging, you will show up more in people's newsfeeds with value, promoting and fostering connection and by letting them know how they take the next steps. What more could you want?

In your sales posts, make sure that you're demonstrating how you move people from where they are now to where they want to be.

For instance, here's a sales post I have used:

> If you're sick and tired of feeling stressed about writing your marketing material and, honestly, you just feel like you want to throw the computer in the pool, then you're in good company. Most people want a simple and effective way to create their marketing that is also easy to implement. What I've got for you is my 14-Day Create Kickass Marketing program that is going to teach you to do exactly that. Simply click the button below and you're off and running.

Contrary to popular belief, you don't have to follow a copy-writing formula in order to make sales, but you do need to make sure you tick the boxes so that people see how you can help. Your posts need to cover:

- What are your audience's pain points – expressed in the way that they would describe them?

- What are their goals and desires – in the way that they would describe them?

- How does your program or offer create a bridge for them to walk (or run) across so they can get to where they want to be?

BEING ACCOUNTABLE

Author and coach Bob Proctor famously said, *'Accountability is the glue that ties commitment to the result'*, and it's true. If you want results, you have to implement your plan and there are numerous things competing for your attention every single day. This means you need to have a way of making sure that you follow through with what you say you're going to do. The most effective way of doing this is by having someone on your team (your butt-kicker, perhaps) who is going to ask you how you're going with what you said you're going to do.

This is where having a coach or a mentor is super-important. Remember, at the start of this book, we were talking about all the fears, the insecurities and the niggling thoughts that rattle around in our heads when we're about to embark on something new? These don't go away just because we know about them. They'll often come back and wear different disguises that are recognisable to someone who isn't in your life or in your household.

The most powerful thing you can do to get out of your own way is find a coach or a mentor who will help you through your limitations, your fears and your insecurities. They'll hold you accountable to *your* dreams, your goals and your desires and do everything in their power to help you achieve them.

STRUCTURED CONTENT VERSUS STREAMS OF CONSCIOUSNESS

I've given you a lot of information in this chapter, but I still need to cover off the difference between structured content and stream of consciousness content. Most people tend to be good at one or the other and need to build the muscle when it comes to creating the one that come less naturally to them.

For instance, I've always known (and been told) that I could probably talk underwater with a mouth full of marbles and not ever run out of words. I agree with every human who has ever told me that, ever – which is why I had to learn to create structured content.

Neither is less important than the other. You'll find times when you open up your computer and start typing and you don't even know where the words come from. It's as if your *higher self* takes over and the words just fly out of your fingers and into the Word document or post. It feels like a stream of consciousness coming through you.

Author Elizabeth Gilbert talks about this concept in one of her TED Talks as *'Your elusive creative genius'* and tells us how we all have different ways of accessing that genius. She explains that some people can feel the words almost moving *through* them while they're out doing something completely different to writing, while others sit and try to capture the genius that lives in the wall.

We've talked a lot about structured content in this book because that's what gets most people started. Now I want you to try creating the space for the stream of consciousness to come through you.

One tip is to look for quotes from other people and just start writing about how a particular quote made you feel, or what you noticed happening in your body as you read it. This happened to me recently when I read the Michael Jordan quote, *'I can accept failure, everyone fails at something. But I can't accept not trying'*. It opened up the floodgates for me and now I use this quote to inspire my audience, but I also talk about the number of times that I have failed – which is quite a few!

This style of post and blog/vlog will resonate with hot coal clients in your audience more than posts that are purely instructional. They will affect particularly the influencer and safety behavioural types, because they love to hear the stories and they love to hear that they're not alone.

STORIES

For eons, people have told stories to educate, inspire and motivate others and we still do this today. Now more than ever, it's important to tell your story.

Your story is crucial for people to hear, because they need to learn about what makes you, you. They need to hear from *you*, because it makes you authentic and conveys integrity. It shows your hot coal clients that you are a *real* human, not just a face behind a name that offers constant advice.

Your stories are also crucial for people to hear because they show some vulnerability. I've had people tell me that they purchased my programs because they heard me talk about overcoming adversity. They heard my history of getting out of a domestic violence relationship when there were times that I had thought I wouldn't get out alive. Others have told me that they purchased from me because they heard me talk about the fears that I have had about stepping into my own spotlight, how I used to try to be *so* professional because I wanted everyone to like me.

Stories help people to connect with you because they will often see themselves in *you*. Share *real* stories. Share stories that are helpful and share as much as you're willing to share.

A simple story framework for you to work through is:

1. Where I was

2. What I did

3. Where I am now.

Make sure you cover off these three points while you're telling your stories so it doesn't leave people wondering!

YOUR WEB OF AWESOME

Remember in all your messaging to keep referring back to *your web of awesome*, that you spent so much time creating.

There are a zillion and one post ideas, story ideas and content in there that will serve you for a long time to come.

Keep coming back to the phases that your hot coal clients need to learn to work through, and remember to share content that ties in with those.

Consistency wins the day, every day

The wonderful result of the work you've up to now done, and that you continue to do, is that you're in the spotlight, you're *out there!* You're *visible.*

You're not in competition with anyone else. There's only you and the sheer amazing amount of value that you bring to the world. Your mindset is getting stronger every single day. The more you do, the more confident you become. You're building your muscle of mastery.

Your hot coal clients will love you because you're showing up in a way that lets them know you understand them. *You* empathise with what they're going through and where they want to be. You show through everything you put out there, that you can help them solve their problems and overcome their challenges and that they can trust you.

You feel strong. You know that what you're putting out there is world class; after all, you developed it! You have developed your own intellectual property and you are a freaking rock star in your industry (and I'll bet outside of it, too!).

You're creating the space for huge influence. You're creating the space for infinite growth and expansion of your dreams.

You're taking a step each and every single day towards you meeting your goals. You're amazing.

You are in the spotlight that shines so brightly that your hot coal clients can't help but look, watch, listen, follow, learn from you and buy from you.

I'm so proud of you.

CHAPTER SUMMARY

YOU HAVE TO TAKE ACTION.

IT'S ALL ABOUT PLANNING AND SCHEDULING.

TRY USING BATCHING.

KEEP YOUR CONTENT MAP VISUAL.

REFER TO THE DAILY VISIBILITY CHECKLIST.

UNDERSTAND HOW THE CONTENT SPINNER WORKS.

HOW TO CONVERT TO SALES.

YOU NEED TO BE ACCOUNTABLE.

THE DIFFERENCE BETWEEN STRUCTURED CONTENT AND STREAMS OF CONSCIOUSNESS.

USING STORIES AND YOUR WEB OF AWESOME.

AFTERWORD

DON'T LEAVE THE CHANEL IN THE CUPBOARD

I have seen the process that I've outlined in this book work time and time again for multiple clients. Every single one of them grew their visibility, their recognition in the online world – and their sales. I know for certain that if you use what we've gone through in here, you will, too.

Knowledge without implementation is like having a Chanel handbag in the closet that you never use. It's sacrilege. It's like leaving a gorgeous piece of art in storage, so you never get to admire it.

You have to get your butt into gear and do the work! If it were 'easy', every business would be out there doing it but, as you've seen, it's actually really simple. It's no different to wanting to be healthier; you just need to stop putting unhealthy stuff in that hole in your face!

Stop a minute now and ask yourself:

- ➤ Who have you got around you to help?
- ➤ Who do you need to get help from to help you?
- ➤ What are you going to do?
- ➤ When are you going to do it by?

It's time. It's *your* time.

Remember at the start of the book, when you were imagining yourself at Live Aid? Do you remember being backstage, thinking about all those people out there who are waiting with bated breath for you to come on stage?

It's right there waiting for YOU. Everything you want is within your reach. Now it's up to you.

The world is ready for your brand of awesome.

You'll remember at the start of this book I had you imagine yourself backstage at your concert. You were in the stadium getting prepared and ready to take your place in history.

I need you now to agree with me on is this: if you do nothing, if you decide against taking the steps towards what you want, it's not going to happen. And this would be devastating.

Imagine if Freddie never approached the band. Imagine if Queen didn't take any risks because they were afraid. Do you think they could have done a world tour with Adam Lambert at the front of the stage, selling out stadium after stadium worldwide, five decades on? Hell no!

Everything you want comes back to your willingness to show up. As Brené Brown says, to show up and to be seen takes guts, determination, grit and courage. These things don't come easily.

I see entrepreneurs get stuck procrastinating, worrying about what their message is going to be. They go around and around in circles, trying to think their way out of all the problems they have with their marketing and their visibility efforts, when, honestly, the answer is in their inaction – or their un-strategic action. This might sound harsh, but I know it to be true for many of you. Because it was true for me for a while.

I have worried about what other people would think of me. I've held back from exploring different avenues and trying different things because I was afraid of looking like an idiot in front of my peers or people who were considering working with me.

I've said 'no' to things in the past because I was worried about the repercussions, but you know what?

The more I built the muscle of consistency, and showing up as me, the easier it became.

Nobody has time to waste on doing things that aren't going to create results. You've got a business to run, clients to serve, new clients to find; not to mention households to run, children to raise and ferry around and nag – oops! I mean inspire! You've got plenty of things to do and, if you were growing your online presence just because you wanted to be famous and be visible, then, heck, you should just go and hire an agent or a PR firm who can help you with that.

If you want to grow your presence strategically, and in a way that is going to create a result for you in the form of *money, clients and impact*, then all that's left for you to do is implement.

If you were to do only a few things for me, they would be these:

- Find your inner confidence and remember just how much of a bad-ass you are. Because you *are* a bad-ass.

You are a rock star. You're a freaking legend and, honey, it's time you remembered that about yourself!

- Get to know your audience. You need to know what makes them tick, what inspires them, what motivates them and what they ultimately want. You also need to know everything that holds them back. Remember, the majority of human problems come from three things: *the fear of not belonging; the fear of not being good enough; and the fear of not being loved.*

- Know the way that your audience's problems manifest in their worlds: from procrastination to lack of accountability to worrying about how they're seen by their peers and what the niggly voice inside their heads tells them at 3 o'clock in the morning.

- Be willing to take a risk and create your own rock star energy. Adam from Chocolate Starfish said, if they hadn't taken any risks, they'd be doing the same old thing they were in the nineties. They were prepared to take risks and to innovate, and this is what has made them continue to be able to fill a room and entertain huge audiences, when some other artists struggle to do that.

- Remember to create your own intellectual property and share your opinions on why your process is *your* process. I can't hammer this home enough. The more you do this, the easier it becomes. It helps you to resonate with the people who are very process-driven, because you can very clearly articulate what your message is and what your unique process is.

- Be willing to evolve and grow (remember the Genius Loop?). Continue to reinvent and dream bigger and bigger so that you can become iconic and create huge influence and transformation globally.

Stepping into the spotlight Nicola Moras-style is very much about you doing this your way, finding your uniqueness, your voice and sharing your passion with the world rather than trying to emulate someone else.

You can do this.

You have got this.

Here's what you need to do now:

Get out there. Go help some people with your content.
Have a ton of fun doing it.

Why?

Because the world is ready for your brand of awesomeness.

EXPRESS REVIEW

I'm going to leave you with an express review of the key points from all the chapters you have read. This will remind you about what we covered and it will make it easy for you to go back and find bits you need to go over again and work more on.

THE TIME IS NOW

Social media has exploded with every man, woman child and their dog striving to be seen, heard and watched online. It can seem like there's little to no space for you online, but there is.

It's time for you to embrace all that is you, and to be willing to be brave and step up the ladder and evolve into the star you were always destined to become. Yes, it's noisy out there, but when you decide to commit to showing up, to being you and to doing this, the world will rise to meet you.

It's the way of the 'new world' and it's time for you to embrace it. After all, none of us is getting any younger.

Doing this means that you are going to take the 'risk' and do things in your way, using your voice and standing up proudly declaring that you are here and you are ready to help your audience.

THE MUSCLE OF MASTERY

We agreed that you're probably going to suck at the start. It's as if you haven't any idea if it's going to work or if you're going to be able to make it work – and that's okay. You're willing and ready to work through building your muscle of mastery and you commit to getting better every single day.

You're willing to do this because you know *why* you're so passionate about growing your business with your gorgeous face front and centre: because there's no other choice, really, for what you're wanting to build and create. You have to be visible and you're willing to suck at the start and commit to getting better and better each and every day.

The work that you do is important. You are important. This is the start of you building and propelling your legacy.

FUTURE YOU, NOW

I've interviewed musicians for this book, and they have all shared that they visualise the outcomes that they want before they get them. There are stories out there that professional athletes are conditioned to do exactly the same thing. They imagine themselves running the race and winning, before they even step up to the starting block or before they step onto the court.

Your brain cannot determine the difference between what's real and what you imagine, when it comes to visualising events. When you have a nightmare, your body responds the same way as it would if it happened in reality. The process of visualising the future that you want is the very vehicle that helps you to align all the actions that you're about to undertake to *that* future. The more you focus on what you want, the more you're going to get it.

TIME TO OWN IT

Far too often, business owners get themselves twisted up thinking, *'I don't want to spam my audience'* and they censor themselves and reduce the frequency of what they post. You are doing a huge disservice to your audience when you do this. You're assuming control of their lives and their feeds and their inboxes and you need to stop it. Like, now!

You need to believe that you are putting everything on your very own: 'Your Name Network' (e.g. The Nicola Moras Channel), like Pay TV or Netflix. You can put whatever you want on there and your audience is allowed to self-select what they want to watch and read, when and how often they want to do this and how they want to do this.

FACE THE FEAR AND DO IT ANYWAY

We all have fears. You have fears, I have fears, your hot coal clients have fears. You can choose to let that rule the decisions you make or you can choose to repattern those fears and do something different. I can guarantee you that many people in your industry are choosing to listen to those fears and *not* take action. Do the opposite of what they're doing.

The key to creating confidence is to remember that you're amazing as you are. You already know enough, you're already smart enough, pretty enough, talented enough and kickass enough for you to do this. We talked about creating confidence, knowing who your hot coal clients are, how to become the rock star and what you need to do in order to become iconic and evolve again.

Confidence is a mindset and is broken up into:

- ► Resilience
- ► Goals
- ► Strengths
- ► Knowledge.

Every musician I've spoken to, and every entrepreneur I've spoken to, has suffered setbacks; they've failed, they have embarrassed themselves and looked silly in front of others. It's all part and parcel of life and of taking risks. It helps you to build resilience and grit. If you are not resilient, you will not make it in business; it's that simple. There will be people who don't like you. You will have failures; it's inevitable. What matters is that you dust yourself off and you get back up on the horse.

It's crucial that you know what your goals are, and therefore what you're working towards, in a way that makes sense for you – and you alone. What your goals are, are really nobody else's business.

Your strengths are going to make it easier for you find your natural confidence. When you know what your strengths are, it makes it easier to draw upon them when you need that extra 'boost' or internal validation.

There are people out there who have a zillion and one degrees and accreditations and are the most *un-confident* people I know. Conversely, there are people out there without any type of accreditation or formal education who are the most insanely confident people I know.

KNOW YOUR HOT COAL CLIENTS

To be relevant when you step into the spotlight, you need to know who you're showing up for, in the deepest of senses. You have to know who they are, how to engage them and what you need to do activate them and get them to do something with you.

This is necessary, because if you don't do this, you'll constantly be busking, hustling and hoping that people will find you some way, somehow. That's not how the world works these days. People are looking for connection; they want to feel heard and to feel like you understand them.

Before you can do this for them, you have to know who they are.

BE THE ROCK STAR

Tapping into the energy of someone who is ready and willing to show up is paramount. People know when you're faking it till you make it! You're not going to do any of that – not on my watch, anyway. It's crucial that you find a way to tap into a part of you that allows you to step into the spotlight and own it. It could be that you create your alter ego, it could be that you find your inner performer and just own it. Regardless of *how* you do it, it's necessary.

Positioning is everything when it comes to stepping into the spotlight. You don't need to be loved by everyone (as much as you might like that). You only need to be noticed, listened to and watched by the people who you want to help, and this is where positioning comes in. You become a rock star of your industry. You have to show your full authentic self, and your integrity and positioning gives you the power to do just that.

You don't need to be on every platform, either. You'll be on Facebook because it has the biggest audience size and it's the easiest to leverage. You'll have your website and then you need to choose one additional platform to show up on.

I'm a huge advocate of owning the space that you're in and not worrying about the latest fad or trending platform and spending a zillion hours per day on there, messaging anyone and everyone hoping for a collaboration. Most of you don't have the personnel resources (nor the financial resources) to be loud and visible on every single platform all day, every day. Be discerning about where you show up and how you show up.

STEPPING UP YOUR INFLUENCE

The big thing to remember is that your audience needs to get to know you, who you are and what makes you tick. Sharing things that are outside of business-only content is oh so important. One of the keys to influencing others is being likeable.

I am constantly pleasantly reminded about this when people share with me how photos of myself with my family inspire them. People want to associate with other people who share similar values and similar interests.

The more you share insights into who you are, alongside the business content (hints, tips and advice) that you post, the faster the people who have just discovered you can get to know you.

Expansion is needed if you really want to help millions of people. You've got to find a way to step even more into your certainty about where you're going and how you're going to get there. It's only then that you'll be able to leverage all the hard work you've done.

LIGHTS, CAMERA, ACTION

It's all well and good to learn and learn and learn. But if you do nothing with the knowledge you have, you'll never get a result.

Planning

Planning for success is crucial. If you don't create a plan, you're planning to fail. I've heard over and over again, the stories of people who say, *'Oh I was going to do that, I just forgot'* or *'I ran out of time'*. They keep running out of time, and the thing that they said they were going to do just doesn't get done. You have a plan now that will serve you for at least the next 90 days. You have daily actions to take you towards your visibility, towards you reaching your goals and new heights of stardom!

Schedule it

If it's not scheduled it doesn't happen. Make sure you're scheduling the things that need to happen and stick to the schedule! Your results depend on it.

Getting your message out there

You now know how to batch content, so that you're able to be efficient and effective with your time. You learned how to write stories, how to repurpose your content using the Content Spinner and how to use 'FOCUS' every day.

When you go through and use all these strategies, hints, tips and techniques you will feel confident to be able to step into the spotlight – your spotlight.

I know for certain that this *will* transform your confidence. It *will* impact your audience. It *will* have you being seen as a rock star in your industry. You *will* become iconic.

I am so very excited for you!

RESOURCES AND REFERENCES

FURTHER WATCHING

Beyoncé says she 'killed' Sasha Fierce, MTV News, www.mtv.com/news/1632774/beyonce-says-she-killed-sasha-fierce

Brené Brown: The power of vulnerability, TED Talk www.ted.com/talks/brene_brown_the_power_of_vulnerability?language=en

Taylor Swift: Miss Americana, Netflix

FURTHER READING

Coelho, P. (2010) *The Alchemist*, HarperCollins

Drury, J. https://johndrury.biz/extended-disc

Duckworth, A. (2016) *Grit – The power of passion and perseverance*, Scribner

Garner, J. (2017) *It's Who You Know – How a Network of 12 Key People Can Fast-track Your Success*, Wiley

Godin, S. (2008) *Tribes – We need you to lead us*, Portfolio

Hendricks, G. (2010) *The Big Leap: Conquer Your Hidden Fear and Take Life to the Next Level*, HarperCollins

Muirhead, J. www.jomuirhead.com

Proctor, B. www.proctorgallagherinstitute.com

Robbins, T. (2001) *Awaken the Giant Within*, Simon & Schuster

Seligman, M. (2011) *Authentic Happiness*, William Heinemann Australia

Strengths Survey, www.authentichappiness.sas.upenn.edu (choose the VIA survey of Character strengths). You'll need to create a login to be able to access it.

INTERVIEWEES

Alexander, J. www.jessialexandermusic.com/
FB: facebook.com/JessiLAlexander/
IG: instagram.com/jessilalexander/

Speace, A. www.amyspeace.com

The Wolfe Brothers www.thewolfebrothers.com
FB: facebook.com/thewolfebrothers
IG: instagram.com/wolfe_brothers
TW: twitter.com/Wolfe_Brothers
Tt: tiktok.com/@thewolfebrothers

Thompson, A. www.facebook.com/adamthompsonofficial

SPOTIFY PLAYLIST

The following songs kept the author motivated while writing this book:

https://open.spotify.com/playlist/7990wBLaaGQVe
Qan4TwdIs?si=Th73VXO8SsKtDUivTrwowA:

Don't Stop Me Now 2011 Mix, Queen, Jazz
(2011 Remaster)

Time on Earth, Robin Williams, The Heavy
Entertainment Show (Deluxe)

Lose Yourself – From '8 Mile' soundtrack, Eminem,
Curtain Call

My Way, Frank Sinatra, Ultimate Sinatra

ME! Taylor Swift, Brendon Urie, Panic! At The Disco,
Lover

Teenagers, My Chemical Romance, The Black Parade

I Want It All – Remastered 2011, Queen, The Miracle

We Are The Champions – Remastered 2011, Queen, News
Of The World

Love My Life, Robbie Williams, The Heavy Entertainment
Show

Don't Stop Believin', Journey, Escape

Fireball, PitBull, John Ryan, FireBall

FREE STUFF THAT COMES WITH THIS BOOK

All worksheets and downloads are available at:
nicolamoras.com.au/intothespotlight

ALSO BY NICOLA MORAS

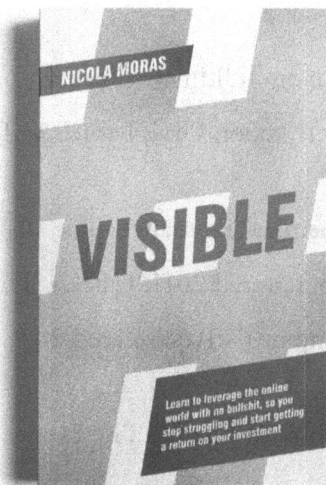

VISIBLE shows you how you can use social media for your business gain. You will learn how you can strategically spend a small amount of time on social media to create visibility, impact and revenue.

After reading this book you won't need to outsource social media – you will have the ability to do it yourself.

To purchase a copy of Nicola's first book, VISIBLE, please visit: www.nicolamoras.com.au/shop

ABOUT THE AUTHOR
AND CONTACT US

Nicola Moras is a self-confessed bad-ass! She's passionate about helping business owners generate results using social media and digital marketing – without the bullshit. This means actually getting a financial return on investment in the form of revenue for all the blood, sweat, tears and money that gets poured into marketing. Over the years, she has helped thousands of people around the world with their social media and digital marketing strategies to create visibility, impact and profits.

She wholeheartedly believes that you are your best and most important asset and that you should become omnipresent on social media. Through your digital marketing efforts you will get results. She believes in the power of you.

Nicola stepped in the spotlight in 2010, when she started creating her own content as a branding and personal brand coach. That continued to evolve and grow over the years. She's adamant that to help you, she has to walk her talk. You'll find everything she asks you to do, she does herself. Her own visibility has increased dramatically over the years and, as a result, she has been featured in many print and digital magazines and newspapers. She appears regularly on

TickerTV as their social media expert and has been featured on Kochie's Business Builders and Today Extra.

Nicola lives in 'the middle of nowhere' in a regional town called Mildura – the food bowl of Australia. In her spare time, she raises her three children, hangs out with her husband, Dominic, and plays and coaches roller derby.

To really get to know Nicola, follow her on social media. You will soon be hooked on her passionate, fun-loving posts – and you'll learn a whole heap to step yourself and your business into the spotlight.

Find Nicola:

nicolamoras.com.au

facebook.com/nicolajmoras

instagram.com/nicolamoras

linkedin.com/in/nicolamoras